Language

and Society

Studies in Sociology

Language
and Society

By JOSEPH BRAM
New York University

RANDOM HOUSE
New York

LIBRARY OF CONGRESS CATALOG CARD NUMBER 55-6003
PRINTED IN THE UNITED STATES OF AMERICA

Editor's Foreword

Language and Society is an introductory but systematic treatment of the ubiquitous and frequently strategic role of language in the life of man. The significance of this role is revealed whatever avenue we follow in studying human conduct. We may concentrate upon personality development, for example, or upon group life or the persistencies and changes of culture or historical matters or international affairs, but ultimately we are faced with the task of understanding the nature of language and its functions.

Some of these functions are indispensable for human society. Thus "a structural system of arbitrary vocal symbols by means of which members of a social group interact," to use the author's definition of language, is essential to the socialization of the individual, on the one hand, and, on the other, a requirement for the maintenance of society itself. Possession and use of language as here understood justify the depiction of man as a unique animal and his way of life as an unparalleled type of social order. Moreover, language often helps to bring together diverse cultures, extending the range of communication and thus contributing to the expansion of community. Students of language sometimes stress its potential role in cementing a community of world-wide dimensions.

But the use (and misuse) of language and the attitudes and sentiments to which it is attached also shorten the reach of contact and narrow the area of understanding among human beings. If a system of language is an essential component of individual and social stability it nevertheless serves to exacerbate social disorder and, perhaps, individual disorganization as well. These negative functions are no doubt exaggerated by some semanticists, especially by those writers for whom faulty communication is the basic source of human conflict and anxiety. This study makes no such claims. Yet both negative and positive contributions of language—to socialization, social organization, cultural and social change, and intra- and international relations—are clarified and illustrated.

Knowledge of the nature and roles of language is provided by several special fields of inquiry, specializations that have been stimulated by problems confronted in various disciplines, including literary study, philosophy

v

and logic, and psychology. While the author takes account of these diverse contributions (in Chapter 2), his central concern is that of an anthropologist and sociologist: the functions of language in the socio-cultural order. Although this subject is discussed in more inclusive volumes, *Language and Society*, as an introductory textbook, is a unique addition to sociological literature.

Professor Bram's professional training and activities well qualify him for his task. Sociologist and anthropologist, in the latter capacity he is not only a student of linguistics but a benefactor of those "field laboratories" where, with appropriate training, both the blatant and subtle functions of cultural phenomena, such as language, can be observed at first hand and often more clearly than in our own society in which emotional investment is apt to be heavy. Professor Bram is an experienced teacher of the social sciences, including courses in the field of language, which explains in part the clarity as well as the informed nature of his presentation and its suitability for undergraduate students.

However, this study, I believe, will have a much larger audience than students of sociology and anthropology. For the interconnections between language and society are an intriguing and important subject for all who are concerned with man's problems and accomplishments.

Charles H. Page

Contents

Language
and Society

chapter one

The Nature and the Social Functions of Language

The Origins of Language

Nineteenth-century students of human society were intensely preoccupied with the question of *origins*. When they studied and wrote about the family, land tenure, the political state, food taboos, or magical rituals, they focussed their attention on the hypothetical emergence and the presumed early phases in the development of the phenomenon in question. It was a mental habit and a literary pattern.

The search for origins was supported by a number of beliefs and assumptions. According to one of them, the still-functioning primitive groups of mankind could be viewed as examples of the way of life of our early ancestors. Another much older notion held that by observing children we could gain insights into the remote "childhood" of the human race.

Both of these ideas have been discarded by modern scholars. Anthropological research has demonstrated conclusively that even the most "primitive" tribal societies of our time are found in possession of far-reaching mytho-historical memories, elaborate decorative and musical patterns, highly structured languages with rich vocabularies, and other evidence of a gradually and slowly accumulated cultural wealth. These findings have put an end to the naive hope of discovering any specific origins from the study of this or that primitive culture.

As for the once-popular equation between the growth and maturation of children and the progressive accretion of social-cultural inventions by successive generations of prehistoric men, it had to be discarded on theoretical grounds as a bad case of unjustifiable analogical reasoning.

Today research in the early past of mankind has come to be limited to those inquiries in which a minimum of paleontological or archeological data can supplement the effort of reconstruction. Accordingly, all undocumented speculations have been left largely to the more daring imaginations of the dilettanti.

This is why in this study we have avoided all statements, positive or tentative, regarding the origins of human speech. Language has been treated here as "given." We know it to be a universal human endowment, we find it in full bloom in the most isolated and technologically backward societies, and we see that all biologically and psychologically normal children quite spontaneously acquire active and passive mastery of the speech used in their social environment. If our attitude on this issue were in need of an institutional authority, we could quote from the statutes of the *Société Linguistique de Paris*, which declare that "the Society will not receive any communications regarding the origin of language. . . ."[1]

A Definition of Language

Having thus freed ourselves from the obligation to summarize various unrewarding speculations on the genesis of speech in man, we can now turn to the more legitimate task of defining what language actually is. Let us not make the mistake of thinking that the phenomenon of language is too self-evident to be in need of careful definition. Firsthand acquaintance with a form of human behavior is not sufficient for an understanding of its nature. The ability to approach familiar phenomena with freshness of outlook and analytical acumen must grow from years of specialized training.

Here is a definition of language which attempts to combine brevity with all-inclusiveness. It views language as *a structured system of arbitrary vocal symbols by means of which members of a social group interact*. Let us consider each element in this proposition.

(a) . . . *symbols* . . .

We know of course that the word symbols means "things that stand for other things." The relationship between symbols and the "things" which they symbolize, however, is not a self-evident or a natural one, such as exists between dark clouds and the imminence of rain, or between high body temperature and the probability of infection. Dark clouds are a *sign* of rain, high fever is a *sign* of an ailment. *Symbols* derive their specific function from group consensus or social convention, and have no effect whatever (outside their rather trivial physical characteristics) on any person not acquainted with such consensus or convention.

Anything at all that can be perceived by the senses of man can be used for purposes of symbolization. Thus, symbols can be gestural (for example, a handshake), alimentary (a birthday cake), architectural (a pyramid), graphic (stars and daggers referring the reader to the bottom of the page), musical (college songs), and of many other kinds.

As a rule, there is nothing in the perceivable physical nature of the symbol that could be interpreted as corresponding to any characteristics of the thing symbolized. A symbol is not a display or a description in disguise. It is always a real substitute for any more direct confrontation with the object of symbolization. In fact, by enabling their users to avoid the necessity of producing such objects, symbols perform an economical function of the first magnitude. As Edward Sapir puts it, a symbol represents a "condensation of energy," and its actual significance is "out of all proportion to the apparent triviality of meaning suggested by its mere form."[2]

(b) . . . *vocal symbols* . . .

The symbols which make up human speech are vocal ones, that is, sounds and sequences of sounds produced by the interaction of various organs associated with the respiratory tract. In order to serve their purpose, these sounds must be heard by another person and must be articulated in such a manner as to enable the hearer to perceive them as distinct and different from each other. Thus speech is essentially an acoustical phenomenon. It is useful to remember this because the vocal nature of language has frequently been obscured by the terrific proliferation of purely secondary *graphic* symbols—alphabetic, syllabic, ideographic, and other kinds of writing and printing.

Actually, the oldest known systems of graphically recording human speech do not go beyond the third millennium B.C., whereas there are good reasons to believe that the spoken word was at least within the capabilities of some of the earliest representatives of our species, such as *Pithecanthropus erectus* (the Man of Java) or *Sinanthropus Pekinensis* (the Peking Man) who lived more than 500,000 years ago.[3]

(c) . . . *arbitrary vocal symbols* . . .

The term *arbitrary* in our definition of language should be interpreted as a warning against the once popular "nature-imitative" (onomatopoeic) theories of the origins of speech. According to these theories, the sounds selected by our early ancestors in their first verbal attempts had been suggested to them by the acoustical qualities of the phenomena symbolized. The followers of this viewpoint scrutinized various speech-sounds for their presumed content-evocative value, and described words which seemed to support their belief as "echo-words." Now there is no doubt that some words in specific languages may have been felt by their speakers to imitate natural sounds. But even these rare cases would not bear out the notion that all or most words used by man are derived from onomatopoeic sources. Even when we run into outright sound imitation we are forced to make the interesting observation that identical natural sounds have been perceived and mimicked differently by men of different cultures. The *cock-a-doodle-doo* of the English-speaking world is quite unlike the Russian *coo-coo-rye-coo*, and the English *whisper* is different from the French *chuchoter*. Thus natural sounds are not really reproduced as much as parodied. They are portrayed rather than imitated. We may conclude safely with the statement that, with few exceptions, the sounds and sequences of sounds used by human languages to form words have very little to do with the meaning conveyed by these words.

(d) . . . *a structured system of arbitrary vocal symbols* . . .

While the relationship between sounds and meanings appears to be free from any dictates of logic or psychology, the interplay among sounds themselves, inside a particular language, is marked by a good deal of internal consistency.

To begin with, every language operates with a limited number of basic sounds (and other phonetic features such as stress and intonation). In some languages, certain of these may not appear in the beginning, others at the end of a word; some may not appear before, others after some specific sounds; some sounds can, others cannot be used alone to form words. Combinations of sounds and sound sequences prove to be subjected to subtle criteria of compatibility, and the whole area can be described as characterized by a high degree of patterning. This patterning is evidently of an intuitive and unconscious nature, since languages, although studied by scholars, have been created and used by ordinary human beings quite unaware of any "structured systems" underlying their speech.

While speech-sounds are the smallest building blocks of language, more important units are *sound-clusters* which embody grammatical or lexical meaning. Such units are either free forms or words capable of being spoken alone (for example, to expect) or bound forms which cannot be used alone (for example, *un*-expect-*ed*). Every language possesses a limited range of devices for the manipulation of both, devices which vary from one language to another. They serve to classify man's experiences into conceptual as well as linguistic categories which also vary considerably from language to language. Thus nouns may be classified by gender, by form, by the presence or absence of animation, and in many other ways. Verbs may be classified from the standpoint of continuity into inceptive, iterative, durative, cessative, and the like. In some languages special forms express the sources of the speaker's knowledge (such as by hearsay, by inference, and the like).

The examination of the body of forms (free or bound) and of the range of categories and manipulative techniques of any given language reveals the existence within it of order, consistency, and patterning just as in the realm of purely phonetic phenomena. Thus here too we feel justified in speaking of "structured systems."

(e) . . . *by means of which members of a social group interact* . . .

This last part of our definition of language brings us close to the central theme of our study. As social scientists we are interested in man's behavior in so far as it affects or is affected by other human beings. We view social behavior as action oriented toward others (some writers use the terms *ego* and *alter* to describe the actor and his subject). Such behavior can be regarded as a stimulus with some foresight on the part of the actor concerning the response he is likely to elicit. This response in turn becomes a stimulus capable of bringing forth a further response. This exchange of stimuli and responses among human actors may be viewed as the very fabric of human existence. The customary term applied to this phenomenon is *social interaction,* and the study of the patterns of social interaction represents one of the major pursuits of the science of sociology.

Social interaction ceases to be a hit-or-miss proposition only when foresight and expectations of another person's response have proven reasonably accurate. This is much more likely to happen between two members of the same social group than between two strangers, the principal reason being the fact that fellow members of the same group can communicate through a common system of symbols. Not all of these symbols are verbal but, in human societies, verbal symbols rank over all others in importance.

Our basic definition of language may be considered complete at this point. Much of the rest of the study will amplify and elucidate these introductory remarks.

Social Interaction in Time and Space

Previous to the invention of writing the exchange of verbal stimuli and responses between two or more members of a social group called for a face-to-face confrontation of all concerned. On occasion the services of a messenger or a go-between could be used, but most social interaction was direct and unmediated.

With the appearance of graphic symbols, the possibilities of communication ramified and multiplied in every direction. Today we are reached by verbal stimuli produced by men who died before we were born. We communicate by mail over enormous distances with other human beings. We have built storehouses for the preservation and the dissemination of recorded words (libraries, archives, bookstores, and so on). An individual can be affected by symbolic stimuli of his own creation. Thus writers of diaries may relive moods and events which otherwise might have remained buried in their memories and poets can read their own verse.

The many inventions for the recording and transmission of sounds have further amplified the already vast area of communication created by graphic symbols. The telephone, the radio, the movies, TV, the tape, wire, and plastic recordings—all of these have done away with or at least reduced the incidence of individual isolation, and at the same time weakened the habit of more direct and intimate forms of interpersonal communication.

The typical alternatives of the preindustrial age placed the individual between solitude and isolation, on the one hand, and close social interaction with a small circle of intimates, on the other.

Modern man (under the impact of such processes as increased social mobility, the breakdown of kinship ties, and the growing instrumental character of human relations) is being drawn increasingly into an ever-widening circle of less direct and less intimate contacts. The cocktail party, where one may meet two or three dozen people and exchange fragments of communication with a few, is typical of the growing impersonality of social life. In a different way, the bobby-soxer who elbows her way through the crowd in order to get the autograph of the crooner she worships is thus achieving an ephemeral illusion of a personal contact. Such stereotypes as the "reading public," the "unseen audience," "the man in the street," and even "public opinion" are quite naturally products of our modern civilization. To paraphrase the well-known expression (originally coined to characterize the presumed shortcomings of modern education) we, in our interpersonal relations, "get to know more and more people less and less well. . . ." The title of David Riesman's recent book, *The Lonely Crowd*, describes succinctly this predicament of modern man.

It is important to understand that amplification and simultaneous depersonalization of social interaction are affecting considerably the very nature of verbal exchange itself. In a direct interaction with someone known for years, verbal symbols do not carry the entire message. The personalities of both participants are known to one another, their gestures and facial expressions supplement their words, and both function within a shared social context. This is quite different from a situation where a writer or a speaker aims at being understood, liked, believed, or even "obeyed" by multitudes of remote and unknown receivers of his message. In order to achieve his objective, he has to rely solely on the effectiveness of the verbal symbols he employs. Thus the selection and arrangement of verbal symbols become for him a matter of paramount importance. We are not surprised to learn that the board of directors of a wealthy corporation may spend long hours trying to gauge the effectiveness of an advertising slogan. Similarly, men in charge of political campaigns or of psychological warfare devote a good deal of their energy to the appraisal of possible or anticipated reactions to their messages.

This situation, considered from the point of view of the addressees, the recipients of the written or the broadcasted word, should make us realize how important it is for them to be able to interpret critically and soberly the meaning, the value, and the intent of the messages received. On the other hand, as students of society, we should try to understand how the personality and the attitudes of modern men are being affected by their somewhat one-sided participation in the process of mass communication.

In a civilization where continuous and intensive interpersonal relations are becoming less common and where, correspondingly, semianonymous participation in mass situations is growing in scope, producers and manipulators of symbols for mass consumption assume a dramatically important role. The relevance of these remarks to the predicament faced by modern democracies will be discussed in the final chapter of this study.

Language and the Scope of the Human World

We have stressed the fact that the invention of writing and the more recently devised methods for the transmission of vocal and visual symbols have extended the area of social interaction far beyond the limitations of personal physical proximity. At this juncture, an equally important observation is in order: due to language, the very world of things and events with which man has to deal has not remained limited to what is physically accessible to him or perceivable by his senses. Once more language must be viewed as a *mediator*, this time not between man and man, but between man and the phenomena of the world. What is more, these phenomena need not be tangible or even real in order to become objects of man's attention. Language enables man to manipulate intangible mental constructs such as change, justice, and function and to deal with beings as unreal as Prometheus, Othello, and Santa Claus.

We may now combine our images of language: first, as a vehicle for social interaction among all contemporary human beings as well as between the living and the dead; and second, as a tool for the manipulation of the past, present, and future, accessible as well as inaccessible, real and imaginary phenomena of the world. These combined conceptions provide an insight into what is meant by the title of this section, "Scope of the Human World." Of all living creatures, man alone lives in an infinitely wider and richer universe than his physical size and biological life span would permit in the absence of language.

Some writers have used the expression "time-binding" when referring to the function language performs in the transmission of beliefs, techniques, and attitudes from one generation to another.[4] This perpetuation of the past is not, however, an unmitigated blessing under all circumstances. Thus grudges between neighbors, feuds between systems of beliefs, aggressive delusions of grandeur, and various other myths and prejudices are perpetuated through the agency of the same chain of transmission to which we owe our accumulation of wisdom in art, astronomy, medicine, and agriculture.

Any individual or group of people who might decide to approach the world in a completely fresh and unprejudiced manner, would have to start by re-examining the symbolic heritage which they had received from the past. And, needless to say, in this peculiar quest for an unbiased perception of the environment, they would still be forced to use most of the basic intellectual equipment which is part and parcel of their heritage. Thus the past is always with us, and individuals as well as societies must be viewed as endowed with a time dimension—biographical for individuals and historical for societies.

The time-binding function of language applies to future events as well. Human beings may fear the future, be resigned to it, prepare for it, or work toward some glamorous image of it—in all these cases they must verbalize on the subject of what is to come. This is as true of thoughts about individual careers as about national aspirations and social utopias.

Examples of the power of verbally perpetuated memories and hopes are countless. Think of the two-thousand-year-long yearning of the Jews for their remote Near Eastern past and their historical home in Palestine. The energies generated by this verbally transmitted dream have culminated in our lifetime, in 1949, in the birth of the State of Israel. The case of an individual life dominated by hopes and memories is well illustrated by that of Heinrich Schliemann, who built his existence on the hope of discovering the ruins of a dead city whose memory was preserved in an epic poem in an extinct language. He conceived the ambition to discover Troy in 1829 while listening as a seven-year-old boy to his father's stories about Homer's heroes. The excavations which he undertook at Hissarlik in Asia Minor and which resulted in the discovery of the ancient city took place in 1871. During the forty-two years separating these two events, Schliemann's life was dedicated to the accumulation of money and knowledge necessary for the realization of his unusual dream.

Language which makes possible such immersion in the past and preoccupation with the future renders individuals and entire societies susceptible to a wide range of man-made anxieties, illusions, fears, and hopes. Thus one who attempts to view the motivation of individual and collective behavior in terms of immediate and obvious needs alone, and ignores the impact of symbolic obsessions spun out of facts and fantasy, misses one of the most uniquely human traits.

That the gift of tongues has greatly helped man to conquer nature hardly needs to be demonstrated—the dependence of modern science and technology, for example, on the printed word is self-evident. However, the opposite statement, that immersion in verbal (as well as nonverbal) symbolism has largely alienated man from nature may seem less obvious. Actually, with the expansion of an urban and industrial way of life, we are being increasingly removed from our primary (natural) physical environment and conditioned to functioning within an entirely man-made secondary world of factory whistles, telephone bells, machine control boards, traffic signals, and condensed verbal messages. We are also becoming used to facing human problems outside their flesh-and-blood context, but instead in terms of legal, political, economic and psychiatric frames of reference. In a sense, man is not at home today in the once familiar world of ordinary physical events: the immediacy of his existence has been sacrificed to the artifice and the intricacies of the symbolic process.

Footnotes to Chapter One

1. Interesting remarks on the origin of language can be found in Vendryes, J.: *Language, A Linguistic Introduction to History*, New York, Alfred A. Knopf, Inc., 1925, pp. 5–16; also in Sturtevant, E. H.: *An Introduction to Linguistic Science*, New Haven, Yale University Press, 1947, pp. 40–50.

2. Sapir, E.: "Symbolism," in *Encyclopaedia of the Social Sciences*, New York, The Macmillan Co., 1934, Vol. 14, pp. 492–495.

3. Ashley-Montagu, M. F.: *An Introduction to Physical Anthropology,* Springfield, Illinois, Charles C. Thomas, 1945, p. 69.

4. The term "time-binding" was coined by Alfred Korzybski, the founder of the school of thought known as general semantics (see Chapter Two below).

chapter two

The Sciences of Language

Linguistic Awareness

It would be an error to assume that preliterate men show no awareness of specifically linguistic phenomena. Quite the contrary, most primitive groups are found in multicultural areas (such as New Guinea, West Africa, and the Amazon Basin) where they have become sensitive to their neighbors' "foreign" accents and to other differences in speech. There are many individuals among them who are bilingual or at least understand more than two languages. Native mothers patiently correct their babies' errors of pronunciation and mistakes of structure. Puns, conundrums, proverbs, riddles, alliterative rhymes, and word games have been reported by field anthropologists from a great many primitive areas. The over-all impression conveyed by these materials is that even on a preliterate level man recognizes language as a phenomenon peculiar to his own way of life and makes it an object of discriminating remarks and manipulations.

Nevertheless, it is only with the emergence of actual literacy that we find evidence of organized thinking about the nature of human speech. Interest in this subject matter usually follows a variety of possible channels, with every age and society specializing in that aspect of language which appears to be related to some vital issue in their life. In this brief study we can merely point to a few phases in the development of linguistic scholarship. In keeping with a study of this kind, we shall emphasize episodes significantly related to other social phenomena of their time.

Lexicography

The civilization of Sumer, in Lower Mesopotamia, provides us with the earliest known texts which can be identified as dictionaries. They are in the form of word lists inscribed on clay tablets, and may have been used as teaching aids or for spelling reference. The Sumerians were the dominant cultural group of the ancient Near East for over 1,500 years until the first centuries of the second millennium B.C. Even after their civilization had become extinct, their language, literature, and system of writing served as a basis for the intellectual life of the Babylonians, the Assyrians, and the Hittites. One of the most realistic human documents to reach us from ancient Sumer has been translated by Professor S. N. Kramer of the University of Pennsylvania under the title of *Schooldays—a Sumerian Composition Relating to the Education of a Scribe*.[1] Written during the first half of the second millennium B.C., it portrays the day of a Sumerian schoolboy and shows how well developed the schooling process had become by that time.

Archeological research in Upper Mesopotamia has uncovered hundreds of thousands of clay tablets from the libraries of the kings of Assyria. They deal with an impressively wide range of subjects such as magic, religion, mythology, astronomy, history, law, medicine, and warfare. Some of these tablets, from the collection of King Assurbanipal (seventh century B.C.), turned out to be lists of Sumerian words with their Assyrian equivalents, that is, true bilingual dictionaries.

If we shift our attention to the Far East, we find that Chinese lexicography can be traced as far back as the eleventh century B.C. The demand for it was created by the intricacies of the Chinese system of writing based as it is on numerous distinct *ideographs* or characters with a number of meanings associated with each of them. One of the most famous Chinese dictionaries compiled in the second century A.D. (under the title of *Shuo Wên*) lists 10,516 symbols with attached meanings and derivations.[2]

Grammar

Grammars represent a step beyond dictionaries. They are attempts to discern and describe structural and functional regularities found in human languages. In their exploratory phases grammars are analytical, in the presentation of their findings they are systematic and classificatory.

The two ancient civilizations in which grammarians were active are those of India and Greece. Panini's famous description of Sanskrit (350 B.C.) has been considered the oldest and one of the finest complete grammars of any known language. Greek grammarians were very numerous. Among them, Aristotle has been credited with the introduction of the distinct parts of speech, and the stoics (third to second centuries B.C.) with the names of the cases used for the declension of nouns and adjectives. Translated into Latin, these case names became part of our own grammatical terminology. In some old-fashioned English grammars to this day English nouns are declined in accordance with the Greco-Latin pattern: Nominative—*the book*, Genitive—*of the book*, Dative—*to the book*, Accusative—*the book*. Actually, case endings and declensions have disappeared from English, there seeming to be little justification for the artificial application of ancient classical patterns to modern English speech.

All grammars must have been conceived originally as purely descriptive studies of current forms. Very early, however, they developed into prescriptive codes for correct usage. In time a conflict developed between the dynamic and ever-changing character of spoken languages and the restrictive and oppressive influences of various authoritative grammars. This conflict arose in all of the nations of Europe, since they had been subjected to the impact of the classical tradition.

It is an important commentary on the vigor and the legitimacy of linguistic change to observe that, grammarians and purists notwithstanding, every one of the many languages of Europe has gone through all the transformations which appear to be inherent in the very nature of living speech.

Etymology

Etymology, as a separate branch of linguistic studies, has a rather shadowy past. Derived from the Greek roots *etymos* (true) and *logos* (word), it can best be described as seeking the true meaning of words through the investigation of their origins. In ancient Greece, etymological speculations grew out of the belief that words were natural and necessary expressions of the notions underlying them. For centuries Greek grammarians and philosophers were divided into two camps. Those who believed in the natural origin of words used *phúsei* (by nature) as their motto; others who maintained that words were man-made sound clusters with conventional meanings were identified with the slogan *thései* (by convention). Our own intellectual battles linked with such terms as nature, nurture, heredity, environment, instinct, and learning are a modern expression of this old basic dichotomy.

While the Greeks were looking for the *natural* origins of their language, their Jewish contemporaries viewed Hebrew as a *divinely* revealed and sacred speech, the language Adam and Eve spoke in the Garden of Eden, the language used by the Lord himself. Thus when Jewish scholars engaged in etymological research their quest for word origins was closely related to the metaphysical prying into the mysteries of divine creation. Centuries later, this attitude found expression in the esoteric system of biblical interpretation known by the name of kabala. This school of thought claimed that every word, in fact every letter, in the text of the Old Testament has a hidden meaning more significant than that revealed by the overt contents. This movement arose some time during the seventh century A.D. and can be traced up to the beginning of the eighteenth century. Although originally a Jewish system, the kabala attracted a great many non-Jews and entered into the teachings of various occult groups such as the Rosicrucians.

To this day, etymological speculations appear to hold a particular fascination for enthusiastic marginal scholars. Etymological evidence is used by men who aspire to locate the "ten lost tribes of Israel," to derive the speech of the Algonquian Indians from the language of the Norse explorers, to prove the Celtic Druidic ancestry of the pyramid-builders of Egypt, and to demonstrate the South American origins of the islanders of Polynesia.

However, in the hands of scrupulous scholars, etymology can and has made important contributions to the solution of historical problems. One of its branches, *toponymy* (dealing with place names), has been helpful in the reconstruction of the history of migrations. Dravidian place names in Northern (non-Dravidian) India and Celtic geographical terms surviving in Latin-speaking lands are among valuable relics of an otherwise poorly documented past. Similar services can be rendered by another specialized subdivision of etymology, namely *anthroponymy*, which deals with the derivation of personal names. The origins of words and terms connected with farming, animal breeding, textile and ceramic techniques, astronomic and calendrical observations, navigation, warfare and similar cultural activities have often proved among the most valuable auxiliary data in ventures of historical reconstruction.

Philology

The dividing line between linguistics and philology has never been drawn very rigidly. Basically a linguist examines a particular language as an end in itself; its sounds, forms, and functional patterns are the ultimate objectives of his scientific curiosity. To a philologist a language is always a means to an end, and the end is usually the culture of a particular society. A linguist studies Eskimo primarily because of its polysynthetic features (that is, the tendency to combine words and formal elements into complex units of speech). A philologist on the other hand might study Pali because of his interest in the teachings of Buddhism, since its early literature was mostly in that language.

The civilization of ancient Greece as a field of study has been responsible for numerous philological developments—among the Alexandrians of Hellenistic Egypt, among the Arabs of the Mediterranean area, in Byzantium, in Western Europe during the period of the Renaissance, and throughout Western civilization as part of the great nineteenth-century revival of historical scholarship. Similarly, the intellectual life of both China and India has been deeply affected by the existence of voluminous bodies of ancient literature. The past embodied in these writings has been held in great veneration and textual interpretation and philological studies for generations have absorbed some of the best minds in both nations.

A truly dramatic chapter in the history of philological analysis is that connected with the interpretation of the Bible. When in the seventeenth century Spinoza, in his *Tractatus Theologico—Politicus*, expressed the belief that "the sacred books were not written by one man, nor the people of a single period, but by many authors of different temperaments . . ."[3], this announcement was received as a dangerous heresy. But the movement of philological exegesis found numerous enthusiasts, culminating in major discoveries made by a learned French physician, Jean Astruc. In a study published in 1753, he demonstrated that if those biblical texts which use

Jahwe as the name for God are separated from those in which *Elohim* is the corresponding term, two distinct and stylistically consistent narratives become evident. The extrapolation of these two narratives from the total text reveals in addition the existence of a third older strand. This analysis of the Old Testament, with various modifications, has become accepted as a pattern for most biblical scholarship.

Comparative Linguistics

In the nineteenth century the study of language was largely identified with the field of comparative linguistics. This school undertook to trace genetic connections between various languages of presumed common origins. In carrying out this task, it evolved rigorous methods and techniques and, for the first time, linguistics appeared as a science—the practitioners of which today speak in terms of "laws" and "processes."

Europe proved an unusually stimulating area for comparative linguistic studies. Within its confines, scholars enjoyed an easy access to numerous related languages and dialects which lend themselves to an easy classification into eight language families. Ultimately, these eight families were linked genetically to the languages of India and Iran and the existence of a broad Indo-European superfamily was thus demonstrated.* The discovery of linguistic kinship among the far-flung varieties of speech—from India to Ireland—made a profound impression on the reading public of Europe and America. Some uncritical minds went beyond the literal significance of this new knowledge and within a short time brought forth a rich harvest of historical folklore, including the notorious Aryan myth.

Language and Philosophy

It would be foolhardy, within the limits of this study, to attempt a definition of the word *philosophy*. It has been used to refer to a whole family of inquiries and activities. Those which are concerned with the methods and the validity of knowledge are covered by the term *epistemology*. Those which explore the most general principles underlying the nature of reality are known by the name of *ontology* (or its synonym *metaphysics*). Speculations about judgments of approval or disapproval in matters of behavior are the subject matter of *ethics*. Finally, theorizing on the nature of the beautiful and the evaluation of the works of art is the task of *esthetics*.

Diverse and unrelated as these branches of philosophy may be, they all have in common their extreme reliance on verbalism. Especially in the past, philosophical systems were constructed in the form of elaborate hierarchies of propositions the validity of which was dependent on the sug-

---

* The broad Indo-European grouping (superfamily) of languages includes at least twelve segments: Celtic, Baltic, Slavic, Hellenic, Albanian, Armenian, Germanic, Italic, Iranian, Indic or Indo-Aryan, Hittite, and Tocharian (in Central Asia).

gestiveness of their verbal components. Language was the clay with which different thinkers shaped their theories. However, they did not always take the trouble to state explicitly their views regarding the relationship betwen speech and their philosophical quest. Indeed it could be argued that the outcome of their inquiries was largely predetermined by their implicit assumptions and presuppositions regarding the nature of human speech.

One of the oldest issues in the area where language and philosophy meet has to do with the fact of the "individuality of things and the generality of language." Plato was the first among the great thinkers to express explicitly his views on this subject. Some historians claim that, in order to understand his position, one must remember that as a young man he had been a disciple of Socrates, who paid with his life for his faith in the affinity between the habits of speech of his fellow citizens and the universal ideals of justice and reason. The execution of his teacher led Plato to draw a sharper line between the world of imperfect and crude phenomena and that of perfect and absolute *ideas* "independent of the appearance and flux of things."[4] In some of his writings he gave the impression of ascribing to ideas a true existence outside the minds of men. This view became adopted by a large body of medieval scholastic philosophers who, because of their belief in the reality of ideas, became known as *Realists*. In their writings the term *universals* was used to refer to ideas, as they were understood by Plato. Actually there is no assurance that Plato, in his discussion of Universals, was advancing a genuinely metaphysical belief. And if his views on this issue can be treated as a purely logical proposition, he must be credited with a useful distinction between the generalized or idealized concepts of objects (embodied in language) and the numerous specific instances to which these concepts (and words corresponding to them) apply.

The opponents of medieval Realists maintained that all general terms (such as reason, justice, and the like) were mere verbal utterances, manmade names (*nomina* in Latin) helpful in classifying the multiple phenomena of the universe into more easily manageable categories. Men who held this position were referred to as *Nominalists*.

Among modern thinkers, the great British empiricist John Locke of the seventeenth century was the first to deny emphatically the existence of universals and to uphold an extreme nominalist position. His contemporary, Bishop George Berkeley, added to his rejection of universal ideas the belief that words of human speech might even be considered a hindrance to human thought, claiming that wordless reasoning would be freer from errors. A quotation from the writings of David Hume, philosophical successor of Locke and Berkeley, neatly summarizes the over-all position of the British empirical school of knowledge on this matter: ". . . all general ideas are nothing but particular ones, annexed to a certain term which gives them a more extensive significance and makes them recall upon occasion other individuals which are similar to them. . . ."[5]

The position of Immanuel Kant, the late eighteenth-century philosopher, on the same issue is not quite free from ambiguity. Although along with all empiricists he maintained that man's knowledge cannot transcend experience, he also believed that some of it possesses an *a priori* quality and cannot be deduced from experience. In his *Critique of Pure Reason* he offers a complete inventory of all *a priori* transcendental forms employed by the mind of man in the knowledge of nature. Modern readers sensitized to the subtle impact of language on thought cannot help feeling that Kant's inventory was profoundly affected by the nature of the German vocabulary.

Some of the leading thinkers of our own time have shown a growing disinclination to consider linguistic and conceptual categories except with reference to relevant situational contexts. Thus to John Dewey language is a tool which man employs in transforming certain aspects of experience into something new and different in accordance with his design. The purpose of scientific language is control and prediction, that of esthetic language the intensification of direct experience. In other words, language must be understood in terms of the function it serves. Genetically viewed, language, according to Dewey, is an outgrowth of man's biological activities. Since human adjustment and survival are rooted in group activities, language is essential to communication and cooperation. And since man's conquest of nature is secured by the process of creative invention, language, by enabling him to respond to stimuli in their physical absence, facilitates the job of constructive imagination. Needless to say, Dewey's position has been more acceptable to contemporary social scientists than any version of scholastic realism or of Neo-Kantian views.

A good deal of lucid and aggressive thinking on the subject of language and philosophy has been associated with the so-called Vienna Circle. Its leading spokesmen today are Alfred J. Ayer of Oxford, Karl Popper (now in New Zealand), Rudolf Carnap, Carl G. Hempel and Philipp Frank. These men are known as logical positivists or logical empiricists. Their attitude toward traditional philosophy is one of critical distrust because of its uncritical use of language. They feel that most "philosophical questions are not problems to be solved, but [pseudo-problems or] puzzles to be [dis]solved."[6] The value of this attitude lies in that it invites thinkers to beware of verbal pitfalls at the point where they are in the process of formulating their problems. At this juncture, one may still have a chance of either overhauling the initial proposition in accordance with the criteria of the scientific method or discarding the problem altogether as lacking in substantial validity.

The virulent critiques which the logical positivistic school has directed against most academic philosophy have not been received without a good deal of bitterness. Logical empiricists have been accused of having "trivialized" the lofty mission of philosophy to the level of a "grammatical" discipline and thus "having sold their truthright for a mess of verbiage."[7] The fact of the matter is that most logical empiricists came to philosophy from physics and other sciences, where they had been trained in the most rigorous traditions of scientific methodology, and that if the demands and criteria of this tradition were transferred to philosophy any number of practicing philosophers would find themselves deprived of their favorite intellectual pursuits and themes.

Language and Meaning

Although the relationship between language and meaning would quite properly belong in the general area of philosophy, this relationship has in the course of history been investigated by various other disciplines as well (the theory of literature, psychology, jurisprudence, anthropology, sociology, and others). This is how language and meaning have come to constitute a separate type of inquiry, drawing on several disciplines and bridging over from one to another.

Toward the end of the nineteenth century the study of the relationship between words and their meanings was known popularly as *semasiology,* a term coined by Christian Karl Reisig, Professor of Latin at the University of Halle in Germany. A substitute term, *significs,* was launched by Lady Welby, whose article under this title appeared in the eleventh edition of the Encyclopaedia Britannica. A more decisive step in the awakening of interest in this area of inquiry can be identified with the publication in 1923 of C. K. Ogden's and I. A. Richard's work *The Meaning of Meaning.*

A recent phase in the development of this field is associated with the name of the American philosopher Charles Morris. In a book published in 1946, *Signs, Language and Behavior,* he proposes a general theory of signs and their applications, which he calls *Semiotic.* He divides the discipline of Semiotic into three separate branches of knowledge: *semantics,* treating the relationship of signs to objects; *pragmatics,* concentrating on the relationship between signs and their producers and receivers; and *syntactics,* studying the relationships among signs themselves.

Independently from its adoption by numerous philosophers, the term *semantics* has continued in use among academic linguists and philologists interested in a nonphilosophical consideration of the changing meaning of words and in patterns of change.

Finally, as students of the social sciences, we should not ignore a movement of thought known as general semantics (as distinguished from plain semantics). This movement was launched in 1933 with the publication in the United States of a work by a Polish engineer Alfred Korzybski, entitled *Science and Sanity.* In this work the author pleads for the wider adoption of a scientific orientation toward reality. He points out the undesirable effects of linguistic abstractions on the mental health of individuals and the social thought of mankind. Korzybski's ideas have attracted an enthusiastic group of followers and interpreters including among others S. I. Hayakawa, Irving J. Lee, Wendell Johnson, Stuart Chase, and Anatol Rapoport soon reaching a wide reading public. Although open to theoretical criticism and somewhat cultist in some of its all-inclusive claims, this school of thought has made a significant contribution to public education concerning the nature, uses, and misuses of language.

Footnotes to Chapter Two

1. Kramer, S. N.: "Schooldays—a Sumerian Composition Relating to the Education of a Scribe," *Journal of the American Oriental Society* 69:No. 4 (Oct.–Dec. 1949).

2. Diringer, David: *The Alphabet, A Key to the History of Mankind*, 2nd ed. rev., New York, Philosophical Library Inc., 1949, p. 110.

3. Quoted by Neff, Emery: *The Poetry of History*, New York, Columbia University Press, 1947, p. 53.

4. Brunschwicg, Léon: "Plato and Platonism," in *Encyclopaedia of the Social Sciences*, New York, The Macmillan Co., 1934, Vol. 12, pp. 158–159.

5. Hume, David: *Inquiry Into Human Understanding*, Book 1, Part 1, Section 7, "Of Abstract Ideas."

6. Flew, A. G. N., ed.: *Logic and Language*, Second Series, Oxford, Basil Blackwell, 1953, p. 5.

7. *Ibid.*, p. 5.

chapter three

Language, Socialization, and Culture

A Definition of Socialization

The child must travel a long way before it acquires all the physical, intellectual, and social skills which are expected of every fullfledged member of a human group. Becoming an adult is a drawn-out process in our species consuming roughly between one-fourth and one-third of the individual's life span. The long years of interplay between the formative influences of society and the native endowment of the growing person, are, in the terminology of the social sciences, referred to as the process of *socialization*. It is basically a process of learning through experience and of social orientation.

Language is related to this process in a number of ways. In the first place, acquiring the mastery of speech and, in more advanced cultures, the techniques of reading and writing, constitute a prerequisite to full participation in one's society. Second, language is the principal channel through which social beliefs and attitudes are communicated to the growing child. Third, language describes and clarifies the roles which the child will be called upon to identify and to enact. Finally, language initiates the child to the *esprit de corps* of his speech community or any special subdivision of it, and provides the feeling of belonging.

The Acquisition of Language by the Child

The human infant begins its existence as a self-centered organism, unaware of any physical or social limitations on the satisfaction of its needs and impulses. Adults in all societies acknowledge the child's innocent egotism and supply its demands in accordance with their local views as to what is proper under the circumstances.

During this early stage, the child is subjected to some verbalism on the part of the adults to whose care he has been entrusted. Such utterances are not, however, aimed at the child as a form of communication, but rather serve the emotional needs of the adult speakers themselves. Nevertheless the child becomes used to the sounds of human speech, learning to associate them with the manipulations of its physical personality by others. Thus such operations as rocking, fondling, washing, nursing, dressing and putting to sleep become linked with specific rhythmic and phonetical patterns.

From the first days of life, the child is capable of producing a variety of distinguishable sounds and monosyllabic cries. These are used apparently in response to specific needs, such as hunger, or to diffuse internal urges. At some point the discovery is made that these noises have the faculty of bringing into play another person or persons, and thus begins awareness of the social use of phonation. Adults attracted by the child's call usually supply some gratifications (food, dry clothes, and the like) and so establish in the child's mind a dim notion connecting its cries with ultimate tangible satisfactions.

Sigmund Freud maintained that the ability to manipulate adults and to secure pleasurable sensations through the use of speech establishes in the minds of growing children an inarticulate but firm belief in the "omnipotence of words." This infantile belief persists through the person's whole life and, combined with other factors, accounts at least partially for several important behavioral phenomena. The latter include, for example, the widespread use of language in magic (in the .form of spells, incantations, ritual formulae, and so on); the well-known human inclination to substitute words for action; the tendency to ascribe "thingness" to purely mental constructs and abstractions such as *culture, conscience,* and *love* (known as *reification*); and the exceedingly common irrational belief whereby things and their names are related to each other, in a natural, necessary, and inseparable manner.

The phonetical endowment of the human infant is that of a potential polyglot. Regardless of his race or nationality, every baby spontaneously produces a rich collection of sounds. A trained phonetician listening to this babbling can often identify vocal elements which have a legitimate place in some of the most remote languages of mankind—from Welsh to Eskimo. The adults surrounding the child respond to and encourage only those sounds which happen to belong in their own much more restricted phonetical system. And as the child's verbal interaction with adults and imitative behavior take ascendance over initial autistic impulses, he discards the "alien" sounds and gradually becomes a phonetical replica of the adults in the group.

Some time before the child has learned to associate sound clusters with specific meanings, he acquires the faculty of distinguishing among various emotional tones injected by adult speakers into their words. Otto Jespersen reports that a scolding intonation attached to affectionate words makes most babies cry, whereas an affectionate tone given to a rebuke elicits a smile.[1]

The dividing line between such preverbal reactions and true speech is far from being clear-cut. Thus a baby may succeed in uttering a meaningful word without giving evidence of understanding it. On the other hand, as all parents know, children learn to understand some of adult conversation before they can speak. The old saying that "little pitchers have big ears" is an expression of this ancient discovery.

Students of children's speech have gathered exhaustive information on the growth of the child's vocabulary, as well as observations of the typical phonetic, semantic, and structural trials and errors that children face in all human societies (although with specific variants for different languages). The critical point in this learning process seems to be the central idea of language, that is the relationship between sounds and meanings. As soon as the child has grasped this basic notion its vocabulary begins to grow by leaps and bounds. It is not unusual for a bright three-year-old to possess a vocabulary of 2,500 words. However, the growth of the vocabulary may frequently come to an end by the time the child is 10 or 12 years old if there is no intellectual stimulation in its environment. Such a person may go on living on this lexic capital for the rest of his life.

Language and Social Roles

Some time before they have reached the age of four, most children become aware of the patterned character of human behavior. In a sense they discover that "all the world's a stage" and begin to play at being mother, the corner policeman, Santa Claus, or even an airplane or a tiger (properly anthropomorphized). They argue with their playmates over the operational details of role behavior ("kings tell everyone what to do," "gangsters don't say 'please'") and show sensitivity to the incongruities of clothes ("you can't wear a wedding dress and stay barefoot") or gestures. The identification and the enactment of all the roles within the compass of their experience are invariably associated with appropriate monologues, dialogues, and other patterns of speech.

As their knowledge of the world and their general sophistication increase, they expand this role-playing approach to a broader repertoire of situations and a larger cast of characters. But it is at this point that society steps in and interrupts the free flow of projective fantasies with practical routines, social etiquette, school attendance, and other rituals. Role-playing ability is not discarded completely but becomes rechanneled into socially designed functional patterns.

Something of the actor survives in most human beings who have had a reasonably gregarious childhood. Frequently dissociation occurs between the verbal and the nonverbal components of role-playing. Most societies impose greater restraints on gestures, postures, and the costume of the person, while leaving the verbal part relatively unhampered by excessive controls. Thus, on the adult level, play acting (particularly in civilized societies) is largely verbal in nature and roles and attitudes are expressed through a variety of phonetic, prosodic, semantic, and syntactic devices.

Language and the Image of the Self

George Herbert Mead, social psychologist and philosopher, has called
our attention to the fact that a child capable of acting another person's
part or impersonating a dialogue between himself and another person
learns in this manner to view himself as an object. In the process he becomes aware of how others see him and what they expect of him. The
psychologist William James, even before Mead, had coined the expression
"social self," which he defined as the sum total of other people's judgments
of what we are. And, early in this century, Charles H. Cooley contributed
the now-famous expression "looking-glass self," again referring to ourselves as we appear reflected in other people's eyes. These three scholars
point to the same phenomena, which can be summarized in these terms:
(a) all human beings are aware of being perceived and evaluated by
others; (b) they form an idea of how they are viewed by others; (c) they
are preoccupied with being viewed favorably; (d) they keep checking on
their fluctuating value on the interactional "stock market"; (e) their own
image of their selves is thus largely a socially produced and internalized
conception. What is the place of language in these typically human pre-
occupations?

Although social judgments may express themselves through various nonverbal channels, they usually reach us in the form of words. There are
literally thousands of epithets, some of which are viewed as more desirable
than others. Anxious to gauge other people's opinion, men become sensitive to compliments, flattery, gossip, innuendos, irony, words of endear-
ment, titles, terms of address, ranks, official citations, conversational undertones, and many other linguistic symbols of social judgment. An
exceptional person may treat the social image of himself with relative in-
difference and disdain. On closer analysis, even those who presumably
ignore their social environment have simply transferred their point of
reference to another group whose judgment they do respect.

When in the process of self-appraisal, an individual finds himself falling
short of his image of the self, his imperiled self-respect may tempt him to
resort to evasions, excuses, and rationalizations. In such a case, verbal de-
fenses become his most effective weapons. An "unloved spinster" is re-
defined as a "dutiful daughter," an "unsuccessful artist" as a "pioneer who
is far ahead of his contemporaries," a moral "felony" is turned into a moral
"misdemeanor." The unpalatable and the painful are verbalized out of
conscious existence and the threat of social defeat is temporarily removed.

Language and the Process of Enculturation

When we speak of *socialization* we are thinking mainly of all the training
and experience the child must undergo in order to become a well-functioning member of its group. Socialization is an evolution from an autistic and

self-centered existence to one based on a minimum of reciprocity and mutuality.

But there is another way of looking at the formative and preparatory years in the life of the individual. We know that the functioning of human societies is not founded on a set of innate, instinctive, and inherited abilities and skills, sufficient for human survival. Individuals and societies are fundamentally dependent on technological devices (hunting, fishing, farming, mining, science, and so on) for facing the physical world and on social conventions in solving the problems of life in groups. Both these devices and conventions vary from one society to another, keep changing from generation to generation, diffuse among human groups through borrowing and imitation, and form a collective possession which every new member of a group has to learn to understand and use. This collective treasury or legacy of technical and social inventions is referred to as the *culture* of the group. Being introduced to the culture in the course of growth and maturation constitutes the process of *enculturation*.[2]

The dividing line between the concepts of *socialization* and *enculturation* should not be viewed too rigidly. The two are representative of two different ways of looking at the same phenomenon. In the process of socialization the child has more opportunities for making personal discoveries: for example, if you hit another person you are likely to get hit back; flattery has a mollifying effect on others. In enculturation the stress is more heavily on learning and imitation—one does not "discover" how to manufacture a harpoon or make buttonholes or dance the waltz or form the plural of nouns. All these things must be taught by those who know them already either directly or by providing models for imitation. Language plays a very prominent role in this process of formal and informal schooling—which basically is enculturation.

To begin with, language itself is one of the major components of the culture the individual is called upon to master. In the second place, language provides a vehicle for the transmission of technical inventions as well as social conventions. Then, as we pointed out in the first chapter, verbal symbols enable man to transcend the immediate and the real. This process does not occur haphazardly and erratically, but within the framework of culturally and linguistically circumscribed possibilities. The ghosts of the Manus of Melanesia[3] and the guardian spirits of the Crow Indians of North America[4] are as different as the cultures and the languages of these two groups. Thus what we call *enculturation* goes beyond training in social reality, providing also an introduction to the world of memories, hopes, and fantasies peculiar to a given culture.

Language and the Thinking Habits of Men

It is sometimes assumed that language is similar to a set of tools which a man can own and use as he pleases to perform specific tasks. Words and

grammatical forms are stored away in a mental "tool shed" close at hand,
to be employed when the need for them arises. It is assumed, furthermore,
that ideas are born in the minds of men independent of speech, and that
only the desire to communicate them causes men to look for appropriate
linguistic media. Language is thus assigned a subordinate and auxiliary
function.

This viewpoint met with partial criticisms on the part of a few nineteenth-century philosophers of language. One of them, Friedrich A.
Trendelenburg, called attention to Aristotle's extreme dependence on the
specific features of the Greek language. Others went as far as to say that if
Aristotle had been born in China, he could not have formulated the system
of ideas which we associate with his name. Today, thanks to the labors of
several anthropologists trained in linguistics, we have a wealth of data
pointing to the close correlation between the thought patterns of men and
the peculiarities of the languages they use. One anthropologist, Benjamin
Lee Whorf, in addition to his investigations of specific cultures, presents a
very clear formulation of the general implications of these findings.

> We dissect nature along lines laid down by our native languages. The cate-
> gories and types that we isolate from the world of phenomena we do not find
> there because they stare every observer in the face. . . . We cut nature up,
> organize it into concepts, and ascribe significance as we do, largely because we
> are parties to an agreement to organize it in this way—an agreement that holds
> throughout our speech community and is codified in the patterns of our lan-
> guage. . . .[5]

Dorothy Lee has applied this general point of view to linguistic materials
taken from the Trobriand Islands (made famous by the studies of the late
British-Polish anthropologist Bronislaw Malinowski). Some of her findings
are germane to this discussion.[6]

The Trobrianders, in contrast to ourselves, are not concerned with
change or becoming. They disregard temporal connections between objects. In fact their language has no tenses. Neither does it possess adjectives.
The same object with changed attributes is simply defined by another
word. There is no tendency in this language to analyze events into means
and ends. In brief, what Lee calls "lineal" orientation is played down by
the Trobrianders. All this does not mean that the group has no firm foot-
ing in the real world. Quite the contrary, they have been most efficient in
their gardening, housebuilding, navigation, fishing, and other practical
activities. The peculiarities of their language are rather an expression of
their world view and their system of *values*. The child born into the
Trobriand society, through the medium of his language, is taught subtly to
view long-range perspectives, calculating behavior, goal-oriented striving,
interested attitudes (such as gifts in courtship), and preoccupation with

self-advancement as inferior to static states of being, unanchored in time and space.

This brief account is not designed to summarize Dr. Lee's stimulating discussion of language and values (which the interested student may read by consulting the references at the end of this chapter). We have cited the Trobriand materials for the more limited purpose of illustrating important interconnections between linguistic peculiarities and specific types of cultural orientation.

Footnotes to Chapter Three

1. Jespersen, Otto: *Language, Its Nature, Development and Origin*, New York, Henry Holt and Co., Inc., 1922, p. 111.

2. The term *enculturation* was coined by Melville J. Herskovits. For a stimulating discussion of this and related concepts see his *Man and His Works*, New York, Alfred A. Knopf, Inc., 1948, Chapters 2, 3, 4, and 5.

3. Fortune, R. F.: *Manus Religion*, Philadelphia, Memoirs of the American Philosophical Society, Vol. 3, 1935.

4. Lowie, Robert H.: *The Crow Indians*, New York, Farrar and Rinehart, 1935, Chapter 11.

5. Whorf, Benjamin Lee: "Science and Linguistics," *The Technology Review* **42**:231.

6. Lee, Dorothy D.: "A Primitive System of Values," *Philosophy of Science* **7**:No.3;355 (July 1940); and "Being and Value in a Primitive Culture," *The Journal of Philosophy* **46**:No.13;401 (June, 1949).

chapter four

How Languages Change

Change and Continuity

The famous statement of Heraclitus of Ephesus that everything in the world is in a state of flux is a truism that needs repetition. Men are incurably reluctant to face the implications of this truth.

As far as language is concerned we need not go back more than a half a century to discover that the speech habits of our predecessors differed considerably from ours. An individual sensitive to the peculiarities of language may be keenly aware of such changes in his own lifetime. As we retreat step by step into the past we eventually reach a point where the texts of the period cease to be intelligible to us. This is true today of a Frenchman attempting to read *La Chanson de Roland*, of a Spaniard going over the *Cantar de mío Cid*, or an Englishman reading the *Canterbury Tales*.

What are the things that change in all human languages? The answer to this question is as all-inclusive as any description of the phenomenon of language. Everything changes—sounds, types of accentuation, morphology, syntactic patterns, and semantic consensus. Ordinarily, enough survives of the past in a modern language to establish the continuity of its identity. The language of Homer (about 800 B.C.) and that of the tabloids published in Athens today are unquestionably two links of the same historical chain. But when written records are absent and we are in the presence of two languages which (on grounds of historical evidence) seem likely to have sprung from the same ancestral source, the two end products of change are often so far apart that we hesitate to recognize their kinship.

When the famous nineteenth-century ethnologist John Wesley Powell attempted to classify the American Indian languages (north of Mexico), he arrived at over fifty groupings of genetically related varieties. Later Edward Sapir, using more refined techniques and a bit of intuition, identified numerous distant relations, reducing this number to six families. True enough, not all of Sapir's claims have been fully accepted by the experts.

The length and the thoroughness of linguistic transformations have presented scholars working in this field with a number of puzzles as yet unsolved. Thus, for example, the ancestry of the Basque language spoken in France and in Spain, the relationship between Korean and Japanese, the debatable common ancestry of the Hamitic and Semitic language families, and the genetic identity of Etruscan remain tantalizing problems in the field of language and change.

The Locus of Change

Having established the universality of linguistic change, we should now try to cast some light on its dynamics. We may start with a somewhat naive question: Where do these changes occur—in the mind of a grammarian, under the pen of a writer, at the royal court, or in the nursery? The answer must be evasive, for changes take place everywhere and nowhere in particular. The point of this answer is that any and every native speaker of a given language may at some time quite unthinkingly experience the need to modify any one of the features of his speech in some manner. His improvisation may be imitated and thus perpetuated or it may be ignored and committed to oblivion. It is as if the social environment of the unconscious reformer were given a chance to vote on the proposed innovation.

Linguists have come to feel that public approval or disapproval of deviations from shared standard speech are less erratic than one might expect. In fact, most changes within a specific speech community appear to follow a recognizable trend. The language is said to be manifesting a "drift."[1] Initiated by unknown pioneers, linguistic changes become a collective creative process. This process has been particularly well documented with regard to phonetic changes, so that modern linguists feel free to talk of phonetic "laws," giving them a lion's share in all general treatises on language.

Patterns of Semantic Change

The somewhat technical character of strictly phonetic changes places them outside this study. We shall instead discuss briefly the patterns of change in the meaning of words, which are more directly related to our concern with the social aspects of language. The words of human speech are clearly a direct reflection of human affairs. Every change in beliefs, attitudes, or social institutions affects words and their meanings in numerous ways.

Our predecessors of the last century went through a long spell of prudish attitudes toward a number of natural phenomena. At one time, it was considered ill-mannered to make open references to human legs, the term "limbs" being substituted. This word is still part of our vocabulary, but it has lost the referential function which was assigned to it in Victorian times. The *verbal taboo* has been removed and the more direct term has been restored to its place in conversation.

A completely different verbal taboo is found in several primitive societies, among them the Eskimo, where a person's name cannot be uttered for some time after his death. Many such names are made up of ordinary words indispensable for daily conversations. Because of the taboo, these words must be avoided and new ways of designating familiar objects must be devised.

In most languages, when a new term is coined for an object, people sometimes take an existing word the literal meaning of which has something in common with this object. With time the original motive is forgotten and only etymological study can reestablish the historical link of the *buried metaphor*. Not many people today think of *spinning* as related to the word *spinster*, and still fewer know that the *daisy* derives its name from *day's eye*, itself a metaphorical reference to the sun.

Words like nations can expand their territory or suffer a shrinkage. The word *fowl* once referred to birds in general, the word *deer* to all animals of the forest. As we know, both are now relegated to more limited categories. Similarly, the word *meat* in Old English was used to designate food in general (this usage survives in *sweet-meats*); today it refers to one kind of food only. On the other hand, while the Middle English word *dogge* referred to a particular breed of dogs it has now expanded to include the entire canine species. In modern civilization, changes in the *scope of meaning* or semantic expansion is illustrated by the numerous cases of brand names which gain acceptance as generic terms, for example, victrola, kodak, and simonize.

Verbal meanings change in *vigor* as well as scope. Some words which in the past designated phenomena associated with stress and strain and strength, in the process of what one might call "semantic entropy," came to refer to mild and weak occurrences. Thus the French *gêner* meant "to put to torture" in the past, and now means "to inconvenience" or "to embarrass."

Finally, the *social status* of word meanings often vary in time. The Old English *cniht* meant "boy" or "servant"; subsequently it came to refer to "knight" and thus gained in importance. Obversely, the term *steward* in the past referred to men entrusted with feudal domains or royal properties. In contemporary usage, the same term refers to restaurant waiters on ships or in private clubs, and only in technical legal contexts has it preserved some of its past prestige.

Change and Opposition to Change

If linguistic changes are a truly universal occurrence, and if most of the time they are promoted by anonymous pioneers, then all little boys from Georgia to Oregon who are rebuked by their parents or teachers for saying "ain't" are victims of an obscurantist pedagogy. This is not intended as a facetious remark. A growing number of linguists feel that any meddling with language in the name of "correctness" or spelling or nationalism is unjustifiable and harmful. Robert A. Hall, Jr., for example, expresses this point of view quite forcefully in a book recently published under the militant title *Leave Your Language Alone!*

It is not our function as social scientists to take sides in this issue. Our job is to observe and to explain. There are numerous weighty (although not necessarily morally justifiable) social reasons behind the widespread resistance to language change, including the following:

1. Since one of the principal functions of language is communication, the introduction of new unstandardized verbal symbols is feared as jeopardizing understanding.

2. Since correct usages are acquired as a result of years of schooling, those who follow them thereby give indirect evidence of a good basic education, an advantage they are reluctant to sacrifice.

3. Correct speech may also serve as proof of "proper" social origins in terms of class affiliation or ethnic extraction.

4. Accepted patterns of speech and correct usages have the sanction of the great works of literature.

5. Finally, deviations from rigorous standards may be regarded by conservative minds as being among other symptoms of increasing moral license and social disorganization.

The Emergence of Dialects

We have reached a point in our discussion of linguistic change where we find two forces pulling in opposite directions. We can term those forces that favor change and novelty *centrifugal*, and those supporting established standards *centripetal*.

Centrifugal forces, when they prove successful, do not necessarily extend their influence to an entire speech community or over the entire geographical territory belonging to it. They may enjoy a limited success and have a local distribution only. In such cases we speak of regional variants. Given enough time, they may develop into fullfledged dialects with distinct phonetic, semantic, and grammatical features. Their emergence is inhibited, however, by strong central governments, unified school systems, military conscription, national churches, and the general prestige of the social elites.

The situation is quite different where a particular area is divided among a number of related dialects and is not marked by a standardized national language. In such cases each of the dialects may enjoy complete local monopoly, and can be viewed as being in the running to become elected as the national language of the entire area. It should be remembered that all national languages began as local dialects and were carried to their prominent positions by the successful social careers of their speakers. There was a time in the history of France, for example, when the dialects of the South (*langue d'oc*) and those of the North (*langue d'oïl*) seemed to have about the same chance of being adopted by the rest of the nation. Paris, the seat of the dynasty and of the elites, prevailed over other provinces and their dialects, the Parisian variety of the *langue d'oïl* becoming the national language of France. The dialects of the *langue d'oc* still linger on here and there, but on the level of provincialisms cultivated largely for sentimental reasons. But under changed historical circumstances the outcome could have been different and one of the variants of the *langue d'oc* might have won the race. Similar developments took place in Italy, Spain, England, Germany, and elsewhere.

We should learn certain lessons from these historical facts. One of them points to the humble origins of all national languages. Another underlines the potential eligibility of any dialect for the role of a true national idiom. We also learn that it is unjustifiable to assume that successful languages have been qualitatively superior to the less fortunate ones.

Dialectical developments become almost inevitable when a speech community is affected by a cleavage, due to the emigration of one part of it or to mass dispersion of all of it over a number of separate habitats. The first pattern is illustrated by what happened to the Portuguese language in Brazil, to French in Canada, and to English in the United States and the far-flung lands of the British Empire. H. L. Mencken's *American Language* provides a brilliant picture of one of these developments and is now joined by Sidney J. Baker's *The Australian Language* and similar works for New Zealand and the South African Union.

The pattern of dispersion is exemplified by the languages of the Polynesian area. The original home of the Polynesians is not known with certainty, but their many languages are definitely variants of the hypothetical ancestral speech.[2]

Interaction between Social and Linguistic Changes

Language change is not limited to those cases where a new dialect grows out of an accumulation of minor innovations. Sometimes major linguistic upheavals are brought about by complex sequences of social events. In a scholarly essay on the speech of Puerto Rico, Dr. Renzo Sereno provides us with a relevant case study.[3]

Before 1898 Puerto Rico was a Spanish colonial possession administered entirely by an imported Castilian-speaking bureaucracy. The garrison was Spanish and so were the clergy and most of the teachers. All prestigeful families spoke pure Castilian and sent their children to the home country for all types of advanced education. However, most of the population spoke a dialect derived from the speech of the poorer and less literate immigrants from Spain. This island dialect, known as Boricua, had gone through the inevitable process of evolution during the four centuries of Spanish rule and was also affected by African slaves and a motley collection of West Indian migrants—Dutch, English, Portuguese, French, Corsican, and others.

When Puerto Rico passed from Spanish to American sovereignty the loss of power by the Castilian-speaking elites spelled the doom of their language. In a very short time the speech of the lower social strata became the spoken language of the middle and upper-middle classes, including college students, intellectuals, journalists, and politicians. Furthermore, the incorporation of the island economy into the American sphere of influence caused a tremendous increase in social mobility within the island. The hitherto isolated peasants (*jíbaros*) of the mountainous hinterland descended to the coast looking for work and vast suburban slums sprang into existence. These areas were marked by a good deal of social disorganization and became centers of attraction for the less secure elements in the cities. After a few years, these sections became characterized by a new type of speech (halfway between a dialect and slang) which was quite different from both urban Boricua and the language of the *jíbaros*. To complicate the linguistic picture still further, the speech of the island received throughout the post-Spanish period a heavy influx of Anglo-American terms. Some were connected with American technology, others entered the island with sports, the movies, the schools, and American administrative patterns.

In this case study we are witnessing, first, an instance of linguistic cleavage along social class lines (under the Spanish rule); second, the "plebeianization" of the spoken tongue with the demotion of the Spanish elites; third, the emergence of a new variant of speech in a socially isolated area with a mixed population; and, finally, the intrusion and incorporation of foreign linguistic elements under the influence of political, administrative, and economic factors. To be sure, there is more to the Puerto Rican linguistic picture, but for our purposes this simplified profile may be considered adequate.

A complete listing of all the social forces that may underlie linguistic changes is beyond the scope of this study. Some of the more important social situations affecting languages include:

1. The movements of rural populations to the cities and of urban populations to the country.

2. The arrival of foreign-speaking immigrants (or slaves) with their specific phonetic habits and grammatical patterns.

3. Conquest by a foreign-speaking group (for example, the Anglo-Saxons in Celtic England, the Normans in Anglo-Saxon England, the Romans in France, the Arabs in Spain).

4. The fluctuating status of regional, occupational, educational, or religious segments in the population of a nation or an area, resulting in temporary over- and undervaluation of their respective speech habits.

5. The blending of regional or social speech patterns occurring in the large urban centers, industrial areas, and in the army.

6. The leveling effect of the new mass media of communication, including the newspaper, radio, and television.

7. The diffusion of new systems of ideas with their specific terminologies and stylistic patterns (for example, the spread of Christianity, Islam, and Buddhism; the diffusion of the ideas of Darwin, Marx, and Freud).

8. Fluctuating conceptions of proper male and female behavior patterns and speech habits.

9. Linguistic nonconformism associated with adolescent fads and rebellion (for example, the language of the teen-agers, Pig Latin in schools).

10. Slang and jargon phenomena linked with social and cultural deviancies (the speech of the underworld, of hoboes, and so on) or with special occupations (the language of jazz music, of baseball, and the like).

Deliberate Reforms and Controls

In what precedes we have stressed undirected and unconscious movements of linguistic change. We must now rectify the balance with a few instances of planned and deliberate intervention into the workings of language.

Striking examples of the latter are linguistic "purges" in the name of nationalism. A case in point is seen in the regime of Kemal Pasha Ataturk, during which modern Turkish society was subjected to the most radical overhauling. One of the reforms had to do with the vocabulary of the Turkish language, which in the course of history has absorbed countless words of Arabic and Persian origins. In the name of national renaissance most of these words were placed under interdict and for many of them native substitutes had to be coined.

A second illustration of planned linguistic change is to be observed in several Oriental societies which are at present undergoing the process of urbanization and industrialization. The new way of life creates needs and demands for which the language of these societies has no provision. This is true of Chinese, Indonesian, Urdu and Bengali (the two national languages of Pakistan), Burmese and Thai. The language problem created by these developments is met, on the one hand, by translating foreign terms into native equivalents, and, on the other, by adopting foreign words with a minimum of phonetic adjustments.

The same predicament will be faced fairly soon by a number of African areas or nations. In the State of Israel, Hebrew has been deliberately enriched and streamlined to meet scientific, economic, and literary needs. Similar linguistic developments are taking place in the Arabic-speaking nations of North Africa and the Middle East.

A quite different type of language planning is evidenced by the existence of institutions of linguistic control. The classical instance of an institution dedicated to the preservation of linguistic purity is the famous *Académie Française* founded by Cardinal Richelieu in 1635. The Academy has been at work for more than three centuries compiling and revising successive editions of the dictionary of the French language. It has tried to be a conservative influence on French letters, but has never really succeeded in putting a damper on the effervescent development of French speech or on literary pioneering by French writers.

Great writers of various nations at times have exercised a decisive influence on their native languages. Thus, Dante Alighieri in Italy, Martin Luther in Germany, and Alexander Pushkin in Russia have been described by competent historians of literature as true creators of literary idioms or even as founders of modern national tongues in their respective lands. Poets and prose writers closer to our time are directly and deliberately engaged in experimenting in their native idioms with almost complete disregard for grammatical or stylistic conventions. Perhaps the most outstanding figure in this category is James Joyce, the author of *Ulysses* and of *Finnegan's Wake*. It is too early to say what effect such attempts will have on modern languages.

Intercultural Influences

The cultures of all national groups at some time or other fall under the influence of one or more foreign societies. In our western civilization the role of centers of diffusion has been held successively or simultaneously by Greece, Rome, Byzantium, Italy, Spain, France, England, Germany, Russia, and the United States; and considerable cultural influence has derived from the ancient Hebrew culture of Palestine and the medieval civilization of the Arabs.

In the Far East China has long been the historical center from which most basic cultural inventions and symbols (vocal, graphic, and conceptual) diffused to Korea, Japan, and the nations of South Eastern Asia. The influence of the civilization of India had reached at different times to the societies of Tibet, Nepal, China, Mongolia, Burma, Thailand, Cambodia, Laos, the Philippines, and Indonesia. Numerous linguistic traces of this penetration can be found in the languages of all these lands.

The nations of the Western Hemisphere have been subjected to foreign (as distinguished from their original founders) cultural and linguistic influences from the very beginning of their existence. Waves of immigrants injected into the national languages of North and South America their vocabularies, phonetic habits, and stylistic patterns. This consequence of immigration has been as marked in the United States as in Chile, Argentina, Brazil, Haiti, or Curaçao.

The diffusion of words, terms, and idioms is a never-ending process. Trade, banking, navigation, music, medicine, technology, warfare, diplomacy, sports, motion pictures are but a few of the pathways followed by man-made verbal symbols in their migrations from one society to another.

Footnotes to Chapter Four

1. An excellent discussion of the phenomenon of "drift" is in Sapir, Edward: *Language*, New York, Harcourt, Brace & Co., 1921, Chapter VII, pp. 157–182.

2. The languages of Polynesia are part of the wider Malayo-Polynesian language grouping. Included in the Polynesian language family are Maori, Tahitian, Tuamotu, Marquesan, Hawaiian, Samoan, Tongan, and others. An able short account of Polynesian cultures is Weckler, J. E., Jr.: *Polynesians, Explorers of the Pacific*, Washington, D.C., Smithsonian Institution, War Background Study No. Six, 1943.

3. Sereno, Renzo: "Boricua: A Study of Language, Transculturation and Politics," *Psychiatry* 12:No. 2 (May 1949).

chapter five

Social Organization and Language

A Definition of Social Organization

By social organization we mean the division of society into social groups and the values and norms underlying the functioning of groups. Our interest is in social groups because they influence the social relations of their members with one another and with outsiders. Social groups may also function as corporate units and enter into specific relations with one another.

Social groups vary in many ways. Thus they may be studied with reference to such factors as: size, principles of recruitment (voluntary and compulsory; achieved and ascribed), the degree of their impact on their members' behavior, and the definiteness and complexity of their organization.

Finally, social groups should be considered from the point of view of the functions they serve. Certain of these functions are direct and openly acknowledged, others appear less self-evident and less explicit. Some writers use the terms *manifest* and *latent* to designate these two types of social functions.

Elaborate social organization is by no means restricted to the higher civilizations. Very primitive tribal societies may possess some of the most intricate types of social structure along specific lines. The natives of Australia, for example, have most complicated ways of defining kinship and in many African groups the entire male population is divided into several formalized age grades.

In view of all of this, when we repeat the old truism that man is a social animal, we should remember that its meaning implies more than the recognition of human gregariousness. Indeed it may be claimed that the social nature of man refers primarily to the universal tendency to structure human relations in terms of social groups.*

---

* For a systematic and informed presentation of such sociological concepts as social organization, social structure, function, and group, see Ely Chinoy, *Sociological Perspective* (Studies in Sociology), New York, Random House, Inc., 1954.

Force and Symbols in Social Relations

There are rare occasions in the life of societies when an individual or a group of people despair of settling their relations with others with appeals to duty, loyalty, kindness, the principle of reciprocity, legal sanctions, or divine wrath and resort, *faute de mieux*, to direct physical coercion. This is true of intergroup warfare, of the apprehension of criminals, and of the manipulation of mentally incompetent persons, including very small children. The over-all place of brute physical force, on the whole, is limited in all human societies. Socially desirable results are achieved instead through a system of references to various socially shared *meanings*, which constitute the framework of group functioning. An individual may be "shamed," promised "prestige," reminded of his ancestors' "reputation," or threatened with "ostracism." The meaning of these terms is conveyed to the interested party by means of verbal symbols, which when understood, function as stimulators or inhibitors of different behavior patterns.

Not all symbols are verbal. The policeman's uniform, the blind man's white cane, and the skull and crossbones on the label of a bottle carry their messages without the benefit of words. Most social interaction, however, is intimately connected with speech and language can rightly be said to constitute the warp and woof of all social living.

Marriage, Family, Courtship, Kinship

As we survey the cultures of mankind we observe a good deal of diversity in the structure of the family. Nevertheless, bared to its common features, the family can be said to be a universal social institution. These common features include a shared residence, a minimum of socioeconomic cooperation, and socially sanctioned sexual relationship between two or, for polygamous families, several of its adult members.

The term *marriage* applies to the complex of beliefs, attitudes, and customs which preside over the initiation of a relationship leading to the foundation of a new family, or to the expansion of an already existing one. A comprehensive consideration of marriage includes as well the norms and procedures which particular cultures may provide for its dissolution. Essential to marriage and the family is some institutionalized system of courtship.

In our civilization *courtship* refers to the relationship between two unmarried people which is likely to result in marriage. There are societies in which the term *negotiations* would be more appropriate. Still another institutional arrangement defines a particular marital union as a foregone conclusion, due to the social encouragement of marriages between specific relatives (as defined by the kinship system of the group). In this last case, there is no special need for either courtship or interfamily negotiations.

Courtship is clearly a pattern of behavior in which linguistic subtleties acquire central significance. In those languages where personal pronouns for the second person can be used in the singular or the plural, depending on the degree of closeness between two individuals, the transition from *vous* to *tu* and *toi* (in French) or from *Sie* to *du* (in German) are climactic occurrences in the relationship. When two lovers quarrel, they may relapse temporarily into the more formal *vous* or *Sie*. In some cases, the more intimate form of address is avoided in the presence of witnesses and concealed from family or friends.

Where wooing is prescribed as the exclusive function of the male, he is expected to rely heavily on verbal persuasion. The range of verbal patterns used by the wooer is extremely wide, extending from the old-fashioned French variety described by the words *conter fleurette* (to entertain a lady with a gay and polite conversation) to our contemporary slangy expression "to hand a girl a line."

Not all societies trust young people together. In traditional Spanish lands, for example, a young man was reduced to talking to a young woman in the presence of a chaperon (*dueña*) or serenading her from the sidewalk in front of her grilled window. In some cultures, the two sexes were completely separated at puberty, and even those who were betrothed were not given a chance to converse. This has been true to varying degrees of stringency throughout the Far and the Near East, as well as in certain primitive societies.

Where matchmakers and go-betweens are employed, one of their functions is to protect individuals and families from the humiliation associated with the refusal to agree to a proposition of marriage. A skillful intermediary has ways of cushioning the shock connected with such rebuffs, and verbal devices are the favorite means. The Bantu-speaking Tembu of South Africa follow a very elaborate game of pretense in negotiations between the matchmaker and the girl's family. They conduct an unhurried conversation about crops and local gossip and casually advance the talk toward the *kraal* of the bride-to-be. Both sides in this process can easily avoid being drawn into a yes or no situation and everyone's feelings are spared.[1]

The restraints on conversation typical of the period of courtship in many oriental or primitive cultures do not necessarily come to an end with the beginning of married life. This is particularly true of those societies in which newly-weds join the boy's (or the girl's) family and thus live under the watchful eye of a group of older people. This is still the practice in the extended family of large parts of India, where the young woman shifts her residence and allegiance to her husband's family group. Her chances of conversing with her own husband remain extremely limited. She owes obedience to her mother-in-law and to all elder female members of the group. Her relationship with her father-in-law is marked by deference and verbal restraint. It may require many years of patient adjustment to and ingratiation with others until a married woman is fully accepted into the family circle. In some areas of India a young woman is not considered a true daughter-in-law until she has given evidence of her ability to bear children and thus perpetuate the family lineage. In some cases she cannot even use the proper in-law terms of address in speaking to her husband's parents and siblings until she has had a child.

Generally speaking, restraints on conversation within the family can usually be traced to one of three types of considerations: the fear of conflicts where conflicts are likely to occur, as between a mother-in-law and her daughter's husband; the protection of positions of power and prestige based on age and sex; and the dread of forbidden sex relations.

The last of these considerations is vividly shown in the case of the Trobriand Islanders, a Pacific people made famous by the studies of Malinowski. The Trobrianders have an elaborate system of attitudes which all brothers and sisters must observe in their relations with each other. They never exchange light remarks or engage in intimate conversations. They affect ignorance of each other's love life. When brother and sister travel in the same canoe with others, all those present converse in a markedly awkward and restrained manner. It would be inconceivable to invite a man and his sister to any cheerful gathering, since no one could be expected to have a good time in their presence. Nothing can be more shocking—and at the same time titillating—in Trobriand society than a verbal reference to brother-sister incest.[2]

Similar restraints were long in practice among the Chiricahua Apache of New Mexico. A boy would not stay in the home if his sister was there alone. The two could hardly speak to each other. If people were telling risqué stories in their presence one of the two was expected to leave. These restraints applied to relations between male and female cousins as well. "A boy shows his respect for a girl cousin by not visiting her."[3]

The French point to the alleged hazards of social closeness between a boy and girl cousin in a well-known saying *"cousinage est un dangereux voisinage."* And in our own society there persists even at the present time in some circles similar attitudes based on the fear of mating of first cousins.

The restraints on conversation and close personal relations between two specific members of the wider family or kin group are known in anthropological literature under the general heading of *avoidance.* The latter cultural restraints are frequently contrasted with a social pattern which is their very opposite, known as *joking relationship.* This term refers to a socially sanctioned situation wherein two persons linked to each other by specific kinship ties are authorized or even encouraged to disregard most rules of politeness and circumspection current in their society. More specifically, they may tease, ridicule, and openly criticize their victim who is expected to take it in his stride and who is not permitted to retaliate. The joking relationship may be reciprocal as well as one-sided. It sometimes includes practical jokes and, between the two sexes verbal obscenity and horseplay.

The remarkable characteristic of joking relationships is that they operate against a background of general good manners and keen sensitivity to verbal improprieties. The so-called primitive societies do not as a rule possess the childlike simplicity or spontaneity attributed to them by Rousseau and by many other earlier writers. On the contrary, conversational etiquette, differentiated terms of address, verbal taboos, and other behavioral subtleties are indicative of a good deal of patterning of interpersonal relations within the total framework of even the simplest societies of mankind.

All human societies take cognizance of interpersonal bonds which grow out of marriage or procreation. All languages identify sets of interacting relatives and provide terms describing them with reference to each other: father—son, husband—wife, aunt—niece, and the like.

The kinship terminology in use in the English-speaking world appears simple and natural to us. In fact, it seems to be suggested by the very nature of the basic human bonds. This feeling is enhanced by the relative uniformity of kinship structures among all European societies. English kinship terms can be easily translated into Spanish, Polish, or Swedish. But the discovery of kinship patterns completely divergent from our own comes as a surprise to most people. This discovery gains additional significance when we realize that such differences are not only formal and terminological, but that wide areas of human behavior are governed by kinship blueprints which are an integrated part of different social structures.

Thus in most oriental and primitive societies the growing child is taught by precept and example that a particular individual is an X whereas another one is a T, and that because of these labeled positions they will act differently in their dealings with him and that he should treat them differently as well.

Our western civilization, by contrast, for some time has been abandoning standardized attitudes toward specific classes of relatives. We have developed the social right to be selective and spontaneous in maintaining some ties and neglecting others. Of a half a dozen aunts and uncles we pick the one we like and ignore the rest. This culturally sanctioned procedure means, when we are face to face with a society which combines a kinship system different from ours and the tendency to prescribe specific behavior patterns along kinship lines, that we find it difficult to identify ourselves with its individual actors.

Similarly, people who come to us from a social world dominated by roles based on kinship cannot quite understand how we handle our relations with other human beings. E. E. Evans-Pritchard, in discussing the Nuer tribe of the Anglo-Egyptian Sudan, describes this contrast: "If you wish to live among the Nuer, you must do so on their terms, which means that you must treat them as kinsmen and they will treat you as a kind of kinsman. Rights, privileges, and obligations are determined by kinship. Either a man is a kinsman, actually or by fiction, or he is a person to whom you owe no reciprocal obligations and whom you treat as a potential enemy."[4]

Among the Bantu-speaking Lovedu of South Africa, the bride-price paid by a man when marrying a particular girl is turned over to this girl's brother, who uses it to pay the bride-price connected with his own marriage. These traditional marriage payments are used to justify the married man's sister's claim to authority over him. Here is a scene which illustrates how this relationship affects verbal behavior: ". . . at a gathering we attended . . . the man of the house was quarreling with his wife about an uninvited guest. In the midst of the uproar a voice was heard: 'This is my village which I have built. I will have no unseemly behavior here.' It was the sister rebuking her brother, who subsided immediately and went on with the ceremonial as if nothing had happened."[5]

Although this short study cannot give a full account of the several basic types of kinship structures, one widespread pattern should be stressed. In order to understand this pattern we must first keep in mind the fact that some kinship terms refer to one specific relationship whereas others are group labels and include a variety of cases. Thus, our kinship language is quite unambiguous with regard to the word *sister* or *son*. On the other hand, when we use the word *uncle* it may refer to our father's brother, our mother's brother, our father's sister's husband, or our mother's sister's husband. In such a case the term applies to a class of relatives and is known as a *classificatory* term.

Systems of classificatory kinship terms, as they are used by many non-Western societies, are a major stumbling block in our attempts to understand them. Among the Akikuyu of Kenya, a man referring to a group of women as "his wives" is not necessarily a polygynist and indeed may be married to one woman only. The term *wife* in this case applies to an entire class of women. Again, in some American Indian groups a man of twenty may refer to a boy of five as being his "father." It should not be assumed that such a man is confused or deranged. He is using a classificatory term.

Personal Names

Personal names are quite often viewed as more than matters of social convenience. Picking a name for the newborn baby and the ritual of naming are taken with utmost seriousness in numerous cultures.

The Kwotto of Northern Nigeria secure the services of a diviner whose job it is to find out whether a particular newborn child is an incarnation of one of the group's departed ancestors. If, for instance, the seer declares that a boy is the embodiment of his grandfather, he will be given his grandfather's name, and his own father, anxious not to offend his departed parent, will treat this boy with utmost respect.[6]

In some African societies children are given two names. One of these is treated as the child's "true" name and is never revealed to strangers for fear that they may use it for magical purposes. The other name, contrastingly, is publicized but with the understanding that, since it is not the child's true name, no malevolent magical use of it could be effective. The Navajo Indians of the Southwest also used to keep their personal names secret, but for somewhat different reasons. They believed that a person's name is a personal talisman which can be invoked when in danger. It was felt, however, that if it is used too often it might wear out and lose its potency. Thus, by keeping the personal name unknown to others, one preserved it fresh and full of vigor.

Throughout the world children are often given names of men of mark. On a strictly rational level, this selection is an expression of admiration for the namesake. But more often than not we find underneath this practice the parental desire to secure for the child some of the great man's properties and virtues. The Gros Ventre Indians of the Plains used to name a child after an old man in order to guarantee his longevity. The Pomo Indians of California sometimes give their child the name of a man whose profession they wish it to follow.

The Menominee Indians of the Great Lakes believe that personal names are predetermined by the supernatural. Accordingly, instead of selecting a name for a child, they commission a shaman to "discover" it. The Ojibwa Indians of the same area expect their children's names to be revealed to them in their dreams. They also believe that some names are lucky and make for success in life, others inauspicious and an indication of a short and painful existence.

To sum up, the diversity of practices connected with personal names is so great that no one general proposition can account for them. Nevertheless, two recurrent trends in this area of social behavior stand out: first, names are very commonly associated with the physical and moral characteristics of their bearers and believed to have an influence on their good or bad fortunes; second, they are treated as bonds between an individual and his group (names may be "owned" by kin groups or families) and as links between generations.

The Clan

In modern Western civilization the family, relatively isolated and mobile, is the basic building block of society. But in many non-Western cultures intermediary groupings known as *clans* form a fundamental part of the social structure. A clan is made up of a number of families, the total society being composed of several clans. Thus an individual is identified with a grouping that is larger than his immediate family but smaller than the total society. Clans are *exogamous* social units, which means that their members do not intermarry among themselves. This prescription is due to the shared belief that they are all descended from the same ancestors, human or animal. In *patrilineal* societies the child belongs to his father's clan, in matrilineal ones to his mother's.

The Siouan-speaking Winnebago Indians of the Great Lakes area are a good example of a society structured along clan lines. In the past the Winnebagoes were divided into twelve clans, four of which were grouped under the *Upper* and eight under the *Lower* divisions. The names of the four clans of the Upper division were Thunderbird, Hawk, Eagle, and Pigeon; those of the Lower division Bear, Wolf, Buffalo, Water-Spirit, Deer, Elk, Snake, and Fish. Clan names were related to the functions assigned to their members. Thus the Water-Spirit clan was in charge of the passage of streams and was said to "own" water.

Each of the twelve Winnebago clans had its own origin myth, four clan songs, property marks, and facial decorations. The clan's culture and therefore the personality of its members were affected by its mythological past and by the characteristics of its alleged legendary ancestor or *totem*. The Winnebago thus lived in a thoroughly structured social world the confines and subdivisions of which were neatly labeled by the verbal tradition of the tribe.

Caste and Class

The classical home of the caste is India where, according to the census of 1901, there were more than two thousand caste groupings. The caste resembles the clan in being a subdivision of the larger society and in that it regulates marriages. But castes are *endogamous*: their members may not marry outsiders. The individual belongs to a caste by birth and at least in principle cannot (in his present life) shift his membership.

The castes of India form a hierarchical ladder and every individual's status is profoundly affected by his caste affiliation. Members of different castes are discouraged from associating with one another. The castes which occupy the lowest rungs of the social ladder live under a regime of institutionalized avoidance. They are not allowed to use the same facilities with their social "superiors," a social regulation which frequently bars them from local schools, temples, stores, and village wells. In the past, the castes of India had exclusive claims to various trades and occupations, which meant that each caste possessed its own technical vocabulary. Other linguistic features of the caste system are caste names, special forms of address, and, of course, severe taboos on intercaste verbal intercourse.

Social classes resemble castes in that their relations are also characterized by a sense of social distance. By definition, social classes can exist only with reference to one another. They differ from castes, however, in that they are in some measure open to outsiders capable of living up to their standards of membership. These standards may include wealth, professional or other occupational accomplishments, education, proper manners, and approved accent and vocabulary.

The society of Great Britain offers one of the most remarkable illustrations of the importance of speech habits in affecting class affiliation and class mobility. Upper-middle-class families often make great financial sacrifices in order to keep their children away from tuition-free elementary and secondary schools, where their pronunciation might be forever contaminated by lower-middle-class or even cockney accents. Bernard Shaw's famous play *Pygmalion* tells the ironic story of a defiant phonetician's attempt to change the cockney speech of a plebeian girl, perpetrating a hoax on the exclusive social circles by introducing her under false pretenses.

The stressing of class differences through peculiarities of speech and accent is not limited to our own civilization. Patrician forms of speech are found throughout the Polynesian area. Hawaiian chiefs, for example, possessed their own court language which they kept secret from the commoners. Similar developments have been reported from the society of Tonga. In Fiji all references to the chief's body or daily actions were couched in terms of an artificial and stilted vocabulary.

In the desire to assert themselves as distinct from the middle and the lower classes, the upper classes in many societies have cultivated the knowledge of foreign languages. Thus Roman nobles attached Greek-speaking tutors to their sons, the upper classes of medieval India spoke Persian or Arabic, and the Russian upper-class members portrayed in Tolstoy's novels converse in French most of the time.

In societies with sizable immigrant populations, such as our own, the individual's place on the social ladder is affected by his remoteness from or closeness to his foreign background. The American pattern is complicated, however, by the comparative social rating of specific ethnic groups. Several well-known movie stars have built their careers with the help of their British, French, and Scandinavian phonetics and origins, whereas Italian, Austrian, and Russian accents have usually confined their possessors to less glamorous character roles.

Deviant Lifeways

It is very much an illusion to imagine that nonconformists prefer loneliness and privacy in the pursuit of their chosen careers. Although such cases do occur, most individuals with unorthodox habits seek out the company of their like. They may give their neighbors the impression of being fugitives from society. Actually they only reject certain segments of the social world and shift their allegiance to others. If they succeed in locating and joining a group of people whose way of life suits their taste, they usually act as conformists within the circle of their new associates.

The terms *deviant, nonconformist,* and *unorthodox* are used here to designate moral labels that majorities apply to minorities which fail to live up to their standards. Examples of deviant social groupings are eccentric religious sects, cultist health movements, reformers of sex mores, avant-garde artists, political extremists, sexual deviants, drug addicts, juvenile delinquents, and the criminal underworld.

Unorthodox behavior and improper associations are for many essentially episodes followed by a return to the "right path." Nonconformist group-ings are often ephemeral and unstructured aggregates without techniques of self-perpetuation. Even when they are at the height of their life cycle, their membership is far from being uniform in its identification with their goals. Because of this inherent weakness, deviant social groups are especially in need of symbols of unity and mutuality, particularly symbols which can be adopted informally and used casually.

Language provides instrumentalities ideally suited to just such needs. When secrecy is sought, verbal codes come into existence. This is true of much of the jargon in use among criminals as well as of the terminology current among male homosexuals.[7] Group vocabularies give their members a feeling of belonging and at the same time accentuate the dividing line between the initiates and the rest of the society. Being associated with the forbidden, the exotic, and the secret, these group languages also possess an expressive and an emotion-laden quality which is conducive to group conviviality and consensus.

Consider the case of an adolescent who is being introduced to the art of smoking marijuana. His sponsors impress him with the expected effects of the drug. Under its influence, the neophyte will become elated, daring, irresistible. The "tea-hounds" to whom he is introduced give every support to this fiction. They also teach him how to roll his own "twisters" and how to get an extra wallop from his "reefer." There is often a close link be-tween marijuana and certain types of popular music. The novice is exposed to *The Chant of the Weed, Texas Tea Party,* and other special tunes. He is well on his way to becoming a true "viper" or "tea-man." We can see in this case how the specialized vocabulary of a deviant group helps to open the gates to fullfledged membership, serves as a symbol of self-identification with the group, and provides an easy way of creating the psychological climate peculiar to the nature of the group.

Language and Law

All societies single out some actions as undesirable and direct negative sanctions against their perpetrators. However, the terms *law* and *legal* usually are reserved to those do's and don'ts which enjoy the support of the organized political state. Very early in the history of civilization, laws en-forced by the state were put down in writing, in other words, were given the form of legal codes.

As of this date, the oldest known legal code is that of Lipit Ishtar in the language of Sumer, believed to be about two hundred years older than the famous Babylonian Hammurabi Code (1690 B.C.).[8] Historians of the ancient Near East have also deciphered the legal codes of Assyria and those of the Hittites.[9] From this point on history reveals a continuous story of recorded legislation, exemplified by such famous documents as the Roman Twelve Tables, the Roman Corpus Juris Civilis, the Byzantine Code of Justinian, and the *Code Napoléon*.

All legal codes are characterized by the fact that certain forbidden, authorized, or required human actions are of necessity defined in verbal terms. Such definition is based on the hope that, diverse as lawless behavior may be, every specific deviation will fall under some "line and verse" of the code, enabling punishment to be meted out in accordance with the tables of misdeeds and penalties. In practice it soon becomes apparent, on the one hand, that every human act can be described in a number of ways and, on the other, that every written law lends itself to a variety of interpretations. Consequently, the ultimate task of the courts and of men of law takes the form of laborious elucidation of the relationship between legal texts and human deeds.

Let us consider the application of legal formulations to a social issue, such as race relations. Interracial marriages in this country are forbidden by the laws of thirty states. The laws implementing these prohibitions name specifically the racial or ethnic groups concerned, most of them applying to marriages between so-called whites and nonwhites. The wording of the texts of some of these laws leads one to wonder how they can be put into effect in individual cases. For example, in the state of Georgia whites cannot marry any nonwhites, whites being defined as "persons of the white Caucasian race, who have no ascertainable trace of either negro, African, West-Indian, Asiatic, Mongolian, Japanese or Chinese blood in their veins." The laws of Louisiana forbid marriages between whites and all "persons of color," those of Oklahoma—between a white and "any person of African descent," and those of South Dakota—between a white and "any person belonging to the African, Corean, Malayan or Mongolian race." The basic difficulty with these legal statements lies in the fact that there are no known scientific methods for differentiating between whites and others, except social judgments based on visible features. Hence a candidate for an interracial marriage is at the mercy of anyone with the legal authority to attach racial labels to individual applicants.

The authorities of the South African Union who have the duty of enforcing the Immorality Amendment Act, which prohibits sex relations between Europeans and all non-Europeans, and the Mixed Marriages Act, which outlaws marriages between the two, are guided by the following definition of a "European" (the South African term for "white"): "a person who by general acceptance and repute is a European" and shall "for the purposes of this Act be deemed to be such until the contrary is proved."[10]

When in the days of the Nazi Reich, Hermann Göring's attention was called by some reproving companions to the fact that he had retained in his employ a half-Jewish general, Milch, Göring is said to have emphatically answered, "I am the one who decides who is and who is not an Aryan!" This assertion is actually less paradoxical than it may appear at first blush. When legal terms refer to phenomena the existence of which is not subject to scientific verification, but is a function of social consensus, an authoritarian ruler may preempt the prerogatives of the public judgment. "When I use a word," Humpty Dumpty said, in rather a scornful tone, "it means just what I chose it to mean—neither more nor less." "The question is," said Alice, "whether you can make words mean so many different things." "The question is," said Humpty Dumpty, "which is to be master —that's all."

Wherever we turn in the legal world, we find the same preoccupation with the relationship between words and human behavior. The American Medical Association recently has been engaged in a running argument with the Department of Commerce to decide whether the practice of medicine is a trade or a profession. According to one study, typical of many such investigations, which covers eleven states for 1918, of 110 legal offenses, 39 were defined as misdemeanors in some states and as felonies in others.[11] Forensic psychiatrists periodically treat the public to "battles of experts" whose job is to determine whether a person who had committed a crime knew the difference between "right and wrong" at the time of its commission.

Examples of this kind can be multiplied at length. We can conclude with the reiteration of our theme that in the realm of law there is no escape from verbal issues.

Religion and Language

We cannot offer an adequate sociological definition of religion within the limited scope of this study.* Suffice it to say that religion is a realm largely inaccessible to direct sensual perception, and therefore dependent for its perpetuation on a continuous verbal tradition. Every successive generation must be *told* about the beliefs of their group, must be *informed* of the implications of these beliefs for everyday conduct, and, where scriptures are available, is given these revered texts to *read*.

Religious beliefs and attitudes are ordinarily first communicated to individuals as yet immature. They have all the authority of the parents' status and are supported by the group's consensus. Those elements of religious

* For a recent succinct sociological analysis of religion see Elizabeth K. Nottingham: *Religion and Society* (Studies in Sociology), New York, Random House, Inc., 1954.

teachings which contain ethical directives often become internalized, entering the individual's moral conscience; those which offer an image of the universe affect the individual's apperceptive make-up.

The supernatural world appears to be divided into two basic aspects. One of them is represented by supernatural *beings*, who possess a combination of anthropomorphic features such as an ego, a name, a will, memory, moral properties, and other psychological traits. The second category of supernatural phenomena is constituted by *impersonal forces*. In his dealings with the supernatural world, man acts in accordance with the nature of these two types of phenomena. Supernatural beings are influenced and propitiated. Man addresses to them verbal appeals which often take the form of prayers. Where the impersonal powers of the supernatural realm are concerned, verbal persuasion is of little avail. Its place is taken by techniques of coercive manipulation. Such techniques as a rule are rich in verbal elements in the form of spells, formulae, incantations, and the like. These are uttered not on the assumption that there is a listener somewhere at the seat of cosmic controls, but that they possess coercive properties of their own. Prayers are a good illustration of the interactional function of speech; spells and formulae are instances of the *magical* function of language.

Verbal elements acquire a highly significant place in the religious life of a society when its system of beliefs enters the phase of codification. Many major and minor religions of mankind have persisted without reaching this stage. Others, particularly those of Western civilization, have followed the path of systematization: they have been reduced to precise verbal formulations, claiming to be ultimate expressions of transcendental truths. Wherever it has proved difficult to achieve unanimity in regard to such verbal formulations, serious intergroup conflicts have taken place. Economic, political, and other social factors often underlie such conflicts, but their verbal and terminological character is always an essential and important part of the picture. The history of struggles between the different branches of Judaism, Christianity, Islam, Buddhism, Hinduism, and other historical religions of mankind provides innumerable illustrations of controversies in which linguistic differences have played an important role.

Summary

In this chapter we have considered briefly the roles of language in the family and kin group and clan, in systems of caste and of social class, in deviant groups, and in legal and religious activities. These various manifestations and phases of social organization, from the viewpoint of this study, have an important element in common. For each of them, whether the extended kinship system of traditional China or the criminal underworld of urban America, cannot exist or persist without shared meanings, without social agreements, without indeed a measure of verbal consensus.

There is little in the physical nature of man or of the universe that pre-determines the emergence of social groups and institutions. History, anthropology, and comparative sociology testify to the tremendous variety of forms and functions that marks social organization. Moreover, social organization represents diverse ways of life which must be surrounded by verbal scaffoldings if they are to endure. This interdependent relationship between language and group life and its numerous implications for human conduct constitute one of the most promising pursuits of the social sciences.

Footnotes to Chapter Five

1. Laubscher, B. J. F.: *Sex, Custom and Psychopathology*, New York, Robert M. McBride and Co., 1938, p. 155.

2. Malinowski, Bronislaw: *The Sexual Life of Savages in North-Western Melanesia*, New York, Halcyon House, 1941, Chapter XIII (6).

3. Opler, Morris E.: "An Outline of Chiricahua Apache Social Organiza-tion," in *Social Anthropology of North American Tribes*, Eggan, Fred, ed., Chicago, The University of Chicago Press, 1937, p. 197.

4. Evans-Pritchard, E. E.: *The Nuer*, Oxford, The Clarendon Press, 1940, p. 183.

5. Krige, E. Jensen and Krige, J. D.: *The Realm of A Rain-Queen*, Lon-don, Oxford University Press, 1943, p. 75.

6. Wilson-Haffenden, Captain J. R.: *The Red Men of Nigeria*, Phila-delphia, J. B. Lippincott Co., 1930, p. 247.

7. Cory, Donald Webster: *The Homosexual in America*, New York, Greenberg:Publisher, 1951, pp. 103–113.

8. Cf. Steele, Francis R.: *The Code of Lipit-Ishtar*, Philadelphia, The University Museum (University of Pennsylvania), 1948.

9. Driver, G. R. and Miles, J. C.: *The Assyrian Laws*, Oxford, 1935; and Gurney, O. R.: *The Hittites*, London, Penguin Books, 1952, Chapter IV.

10. Bauer, Anne: "South Africa's New Racial Order," *The American Scholar*, 21:No.1:35 (Winter 1951–52).

11. Queen, S. A.: *The Passing of the County Jail*, Menasha, Wis., George Banta Publishing Company, 1920, pp. 75–82.

chapter six

Languages in the Life of Nations

National States and Ethnic Groups

In our present-day civilization, the most effective large units of social solidarity are those which are founded on the national principle. They belong to two basic varieties: self-governing territorial national states and politically unorganized ethnic societies.

The dividing line between these two is not always clear-cut nor fixed for all time. Thus, in recent times, several formerly dependent ethnic societies have succeeded in changing their status to that of nation-states. On the other hand, history is rich in examples of national states which have been reduced over a period of years to the level of ethnic groupings.

Previous to 1918, the Estonians, for example, never existed as a nation-state, but lived successively under the rule of Denmark, the Livonian Order, Sweden, and Russia. In 1918, however, Estonia became a full-fledged sovereign nation with all the attributes of the modern political state.* The Welsh, on the other hand, had existed as an independent nation, ruled by its own kings, until 1282, but since then have declined to the rank of an ethnic minority within the body politic of the British Kingdom.

The sentiments of unity and solidarity underlying the existence of nation-states and ethnic societies differ significantly in some of their properties. An ethnic grouping exists in virtue of a shared cultural tradition, an image of common destiny, and of feelings of spiritual kinship, all of which may survive in the absence of a commonly shared territory and political organization. The unity of an ethnic grouping has a familylike quality, frequently marked by semibiological undertones. This description fits the case of the Armenians, who whether living under Turkish or Russian rule, or in dispersion in the countries of the Near East, Europe, and the Western Hemisphere, have for centuries preserved a feeling of group unity and attitudes of solidarity and mutuality.

A political nation-state, in contrast to ethnic groups, is often less homogeneous in composition and less well supported by sentiments of biological kinship and spiritual togetherness among its members. It easily

---

* At present Estonia is one of the captive nations ruled by the Soviet military power.

49

compensates for the absence of such "organic" ties by stressing outward symbols of national sovereignty and by encouraging training in the duties of citizenship.

The nation-state and the ethnic society sometimes eye each other with feelings of envy. Dependent and at times landless ethnic minorities may be attracted by the prestige, the authority, and the power structure of sovereign nations. Nation-states, on the other hand, are anxious to achieve the inwardness and authenticity of national sentiments which animate the existence of ethnic groupings.

Both these forms of national existence are intimately associated in men's minds with verbal symbols. In fact, their very survival can hardly be imagined in the absence of verbal reinforcements. Let us consider some of these linguistic ingredients in the complex of national phenomena.

National Names and Geographical Symbols

A human aggregate with any claims to national existence (of either of the two types described above) must have a *name*. How could its members identify themselves or be identified by others in the absence of a recognized group label? The denial of a name to a national minority is a tested administrative technique aimed at the eventual obliteration of its identity. For example, the part of divided Poland which was under Russian rule was between 1863 and 1917 officially termed the Vistula Region thus doing away with the very name of the nation.

On the other hand, an artificially coined name may in a short time intensify previously latent feelings of national unity. A recent and spectacular illustration of this process is provided by the success of the synthetic name of Pakistan, founded as a sovereign nation in 1947. This name had been coined in 1933 by Choudhary Rahmat Ali, who intended P to stand for Punjab, A for the Afghan border provinces, K for Kashmir, S for Sind and *tan* for Baluchistan. The nation, as it is formed now, also includes the province of Bengal (where the majority of its population resides) but has failed to incorporate the province of Kashmir, which has remained under the *de facto* rule of India. With all these modifications, Pakistan has achieved within a few years a reasonable semblance of national unity, with its youth and leadership turning an artificial name into a psychological reality.

In addition to names, national collectivities, as a rule, are associated with specific geographical boundaries or landmarks, past or present. The linkage between nation-states and the territories over which they hold sway is in no need of elaboration. Less well known are the cases of groups which have preserved the memories of their past residence. In this manner, the Arabs of Morocco include in their history the period during which they ruled over the Iberian peninsula. Some of the old Moroccan families even preserve the keys from their "homes" in Spain.

Names of geographical features often become rallying points for group emotions. Passions aroused by references to such names may far exceed the practical value of the areas involved. Thus violent demonstrations resulting in casualties took place in Italy in recent years in connection with the political status of the port of Trieste, although unbiased experts maintain that Trieste has a very limited economic or strategic value today. This aspect of the issue, however, is past the point of cold reasoning now that Trieste has become a *sacred name*. Similarly sacred at different times have been such names as Vilna (or Wilno), claimed simultaneously by the Poles and the Lithuanians, Alsace-Lorraine, which was contended for by France and Germany, and the symbolic fortress of Gibraltar, the crown colony of Great Britain, the return of which is demanded by Spain today.

National Heroes, Traits, Literature, and Folklore

The vocabulary of terms capable of arousing national emotions is not limited to geographical references, but includes commonly the names of men or women who, for one reason or another, have become symbols of group pride: Joan of Arc, Wilhelm Tell, Mahatma Gandhi, Garibaldi, and many others. The legends surrounding such national heroes frequently embody culturally accented and highly valued character traits.

Moreover, nations and ethnic groups often view themselves as possessed of specific psychological traits, sometimes regarding them as part of their biological heritage. Interestingly enough, these are not limited to self-praise, but also include shortcomings which are sometimes acknowledged with an attitude of amused pride. For example, Russians used to say proudly that "our land is vast and wealthy but there is no order in it," and Irish are known to make smiling references to their fighting qualities. National self-characterizations are often expressed in a laconic and stereotyped manner and become stable components in national vocabularies. Beliefs regarding alleged national "roles" or "missions" and associated sayings and clichés are closely related to national self-characterizations.

Names of national foods and drinks with their power to evoke the family circle, occasions of commensality, and the sharing of taste among fellow nationals, should not be ignored because of their less lofty nature. It is no accident that in describing homesickness among Americans in uniform in foreign lands, it was—and, to some extent, is—common to speak of mother's apple pie, sodas in the corner drugstore, and coffee and doughnuts at a road stand.

And last but not least we should point to national legacies of songs, dances, games, proverbs, rhymes, sayings, plays, stories, novels, and poems. By portraying, stylizing, and condensing true or idealized national lifeways and by providing occasions for shared pastimes, such legacies serve as important "spiritual homes" for human groups.

National Emotions

Those historians and social scientists who have tried to view national or ethnic continuities in terms of economic or geographical factors alone, have failed to realize the extent to which systems of shared symbols and emotions can override, for better or for worse, considerations of material self-interest. We are dealing here with verbal labels capable of arousing strong collective emotions, and with collective emotions perpetuated through the use of these labels. As we pointed out in the beginning of this study, human societies do not react to the real, the immediate and the present alone, but function as well in terms of *social memories*.

In order to appreciate the depth of human attachment to native speech, it should be remembered that the thrill of discovering and *naming* the phenomena of the world happens but once in each person's lifetime. Whatever other languages a person may learn subsequently, they cannot have the depth of emotional associations possessed by the speech of early childhood. The *mother tongue, Muttersprache, mame loshen* (in Yiddish), and *langue maternelle* are as deeply imbedded in our inner worlds as our first infantile loves or, in the Freudian framework, our Oedipal involvements.

The Battle of Languages: the Case of India

India provides an excellent illustration of the intricate tie between the distribution of languages and the power structure within a given society. By the time the British East India Company made its appearance in the seventeenth century, India had gone through more than three thousand years of advanced civilization. Traders, soldiers, and administrators from Great Britain found a multitude of ethnic and national groups, using numerous languages, many of which had systems of writing and rich literary traditions. However, it was not before the beginning of the nineteenth century that the British were called upon to make an important decision involving the social functions of some of these languages.

This decision took place in connection with the proposed reform of the educational system of India. The British had become aware of the fact that the influential educated classes of India were looking down upon the vernaculars spoken by the masses of people, reserving their respect for literacy in Arabic, Persian, or Sanscrit. A minority among Indian literati was in favor of the living speech of the people, but even they felt that most prerequisites to public education in vernaculars were absent. A compromise was struck by selecting English.

This conflict is known as the struggle of orientalists and anglicists. It was resolved by Lord Macaulay's Minute in favor of the anglicists, promulgated in 1835. From this date to the declaration of Indian independence, English became the principal language of instruction, while local vernaculars were used in the lower grades, thus gradually preparing the reading public for publications in vernacular speech. By the end of the nineteenth century English had fulfilled its major function as a vehicle for the introduction of European ideas and techniques and England, in a sense, prepared its own exit by training native Indians in the skills of modern statehood.

The leaders of the Indian struggle for national independence, over and above their concerted efforts directed against the British rule, had to face the problem of national disunity. The latter was especially aggravated by two factors: the split between the Hinduist majority and the Mohammedan minority, and the multiplicity of languages and dialects conducive to parochialism and conflicts.

The Hinduist-Mohammedan rift had distinct linguistic undertones as well. Islamic influences had served as a channel for the intrusion into various languages of India of words and forms borrowed from Arabic, Persian, and Turkic languages. Some predominantly Mohammedan areas adopted the Persian variety of the Arabic script, thereby making their writing unintelligible to those Hindus who were trained in the traditional script of India (*Nagari* or *Deva Nagari*). Thus the W. Hindi language of Northern India became split into the Muslim variety (known as Urdu) and the Hinduist variety (or Hindi). The leaders of the Hinduist faction carried their opposition to Urdu a step further by purging their speech (Hindi) of all terms of Muslim origin. Hindustani, a dialect of Hindi, in use in the Upper Gangetic Doab and in the Eastern Punjab, appeared at this juncture as the only linguistic bridge between the heavily arabized Urdu and the similarly sanscritized Hindi. Hindustani could be written in both the Persian and the Nagari scripts, and had a balanced assortment of Arabic, Persian, and Sanscrit words. When the leaders of the nationalist movement met in Calcutta in 1916, they decided to back Hindustani as the language of national emancipation and national unity.

As we know, India succeeded in achieving political independence not as a united nation but in the form of the two antagonistic nation-states of Mohammedan Pakistan and Hinduist India. Hindustani, which had been slated as a symbol of national unity, lost its function and relapsed into its former status of a regional language. Urdu became the official national language of Pakistan, and Hindi was chosen for this role by India.

This division, however, did not put an end to the operation of centrifugal forces in either Pakistan or India. Pakistan as a nation is made up of the two geographically unconnected areas of Western Pakistan and the Province of Bengal. The governing elites and the fountainhead of Islamic nationalism are in Urdu-speaking Western Pakistan, but the majority of the population and most of the natural wealth are concentrated in Bengali-speaking Bengal. For a while Urdu was the only official language in both parts of the new state, but recently Bengal asserted itself against the domination of Urdu, and after several severe riots secured the right of linguistic equality. In this way Pakistan became a bilingual state, with considerable bitterness on both sides.

India is at present going through a very similar conflict, aggravated by the wider range of languages and local loyalties. The majority of the population of India is divided among numerous large and small Indo-European languages. However, southern India is inhabited by over seventy million speakers of the Dravidian language family. The Dravidians feel that they are not getting their share of participation in national administration. Besides they are reluctant to adopt Hindi as the coming language of Indian national unity. Within the Dravidian camp there is disunity too, with local pressure groups claiming autonomy along linguistic lines.

The issue came to a climax with the death through self-imposed fasting of the leader of the Telugu language movement in the province of Madras. The government was forced to give in to popular pressures, and the predominantly Telugu-speaking state was inaugurated in October 1953 under the name of Andhra. The boundary runs through the city of Madras itself. The new state has a population of 21,500,000 and is already exerting an attraction on some Telugu-speaking groups left outside its limits. The surrender of the central government to the principle of linguistic self-determination was at once followed by campaigns in other areas of India, such as the Southern Bombay province where the majority speaks Kanarese (also a Dravidian tongue). The next few decades will show whether a *modus vivendi* can be worked out between the centrifugal ethnic-linguistic forces and the ideal of national unity. In the meantime, even the parliament of India is reduced to using English as the language of deliberations, even though not more than five per cent of the total population of the nation has adequate knowledge of it.

Multilingual Nations and Their Problems

The coexistence of several unrelated languages under the same national roof is by no means an Indian monopoly, as the following cases illustrate.

In Burma, according to the census of 1931, only 67 per cent of the population spoke Burmese, the official language of the country. The remaining third of the nation were divided among more than one hundred different languages and dialects belonging to half a dozen language families. The immigrants from India and China spoke several languages of their respective homelands, and the educated classes of the nation were fluent in English.

The Philippine nation is similarly fragmented into numerous speech communities—eighty-seven, according to one authority.[1] Fortunately, almost all of these belong to the same Malayo-Polynesian language family. The government is encouraging one of the most frequently used dialects,

Tagalog, to play the role of the national language. Finally, the educated classes have a fairly good knowledge of Spanish and English.

In Mexico, according to the national census of 1940, almost 15 per cent of the total population (five years of age or over) spoke one of the many Indian languages. Half of these native speakers did not know any Spanish at all.

The Gold Coast in West Africa is of great interest to the social scientist since it seems to be on the threshold of political independence and exemplifies one of the most significant experiments in native self-rule in Africa. The government of this young nation faces a population of about four million, divided into some sixteen native speech communities. The literate classes of the nation have shown great enthusiasm for the use of English, and there are currently published more than twelve English newspapers in this country.

Another African area fast moving toward self-rule is Nigeria. There the population is divided into six major language groups (Hausa, Yoruba, Ibo, Kanuri, Fula, and Efik-Ibibio), constituting about 85 per cent of the total. The remaining 15 per cent of the population is distributed among some forty smaller language communities.

These countries—Burma, the Philippine Republic, Mexico, Gold Coast, and Nigeria—are but five of the several instances in the contemporary world that illustrate the broad diffusion of the problem of multilingualism.

As long as the Igorot of Luzon, the Maya of Yucatan, or the Dagomba of the Gold Coast remained in isolation from the rest of mankind, with most of their needs satisfied by local means, the smallness of their speech communities was of little significance. The introduction of modern means of communication and transportation, combined with other forces of modern economy and of present-day political and strategic developments, are drawing them into direct contacts with the affairs of the world. They are becoming aware that literacy is of great importance in their new role. And it is at this juncture that the question arises—literacy in what language?

There are disadvantages to whatever answer is given to this question. If the group chooses to receive instruction in the idiom which they speak, certain crucial questions arise. How and where should the required number of teachers be trained? What will the natives read after having mastered the limited elementary manuals prepared for them? How far, in other words, will the newly acquired literacy take them toward their goal of direct communication with the world?

An alternative might be found in the adoption of the most widely used language of a given broad area. But this solution carries with it the danger of political domination by the favored group, and the fear of gradual obliteration of the less favored small speech communities. Moreover, as in the case of the first alternative, such a program does not seem to lessen the apprehension that the main objective, that is, joining the "universal discourse," will be unachieved, since even the most popular language in a preindustrial society is likely to be deprived of the technical and scientific equipment needed to catch up with the progress of mankind in these areas.

A third, so-called "colonial," solution would mean the adoption of a foreign language of an advanced European nation, such as English, French, or Italian. This plan, of course, would simplify access to the accumulated knowledge of the West. But the obvious practical advantages would be to some extent neutralized by the culturally alienating effect of a European language on native elites, induced to read European literature, to think in terms of European concepts and categories, and to speak an idiom uncomfortably reminiscent of colonial regimes.

Not many students realize that at the birth of the United States it was felt by some that the new nation needed a language of its own. The great American lexicographer Noah Webster, for example, expressed this view, writing: "As an independent nation, our honor requires us to have a system of our own, in language as well as in government. Great Britain whose children we are, and whose language we speak, should no longer be our standard; for the taste of her writers is already corrupted and her language on the decline. . . ."[2] These lines should help us to understand the reluctance of Asiatic or African societies to solve their linguistic problems by adopting any of the well-equipped languages of Europe.

Makeshift Languages

When European explorers and settlers first came into direct contact with the populations of recently discovered lands, they were inclined to view the natives as childlike, barbarous, and intellectually inferior. When individual natives made their first attempts to imitate and learn the speech of the dominant group, the Europeans were not surprised to hear their languages simplified and distorted. Instead of offering instruction in the correct use of their speech, they condescendingly accepted the natives' mangled versions as good enough for all practical purposes. In time, the natives began to use these makeshift languages to communicate with other natives from distant areas with whom they were thrown together on the white man's plantations and in white settlements. In this way, what began as a kind of baby talk for the benefit of presumably retarded learners soon developed into well-functioning languages covering wide territories.

The vocabulary of these languages was as a rule based on borrowings from the speech of Europeans. Native terms were added to designate indigenous plants, animals, foods, and similar items. The grammar was characterized by extreme simplicity, with declensions and conjugations eliminated and the word order stressing vigor rather than shades of meaning.

In some cases the function of such makeshift languages remained limited to their role as a *lingua franca* between two or more alien groups. In certain situations, however, they were substituted for the original speech of a native group and became its only medium of expression. Linguists use the term *creolized* in referring to makeshift languages adopted as their only form of speech by native populations.

Haitian Creole is one of the most successful and best-known examples of a creolized language. It is the native speech of almost the entire population of the Republic of Haiti, a nation of over three million according to the census of 1951. Haitian Creole is derived from seventeenth- and eighteenth-century French with the addition of morphological and syntactic elements contributed by the West African languages spoken by the many slaves brought to this part of the new Western world.[3]

Another well-known creolized language is the Mauritius Creole which came into existence on the island of Mauritius (formerly known as Ile de France) in the Indian Ocean as a means of communication between the Malagasy slaves imported from Madagascar and their French masters. The French had occupied this island between 1715 and 1810, when it was taken over by the British. Under British rule masses of coolie laborers were brought from India. But Mauritius Creole survived these changes and is still in use as the native speech among the descendants of the Malagasy slaves. Students of this makeshift language have commented on its expressive quality and have even voiced their regrets about the encroachment of standard French which is taught in the schools of the island.[4]

Two further illustrations of widely adopted makeshift languages are the creolized Portuguese which was spoken until the turn of the century on the Island of San Thomé by the descendants of runaway slaves, and a creolized variety of Dutch that evolved in earlier years on the Virgin Islands.

Among makeshift languages which never became adopted as native idioms by any groups, are such pidgin tongues as the following:

1. the pidgin English in use along the coast of China and in the ports of Southeast Asia, Formosa, Korea, and Japan;

2. the Melanesian pidgin English (sometimes referred to as Beach-la-Mar or Sandalwood English) used between whites and natives or between natives from different speech communities in the vast island area about New Guinea;[5]

3. the West-Coast pidgin English of Sierra Leone and Gambia of West Africa;

4. the "Kru-boy" pidgin, based on a mixture of English and Kru languages in use among cabin boys, sailors, traders, and others along the west coast of Africa;

5. *Le Petit-Nègre* spoken mostly in the French possessions of West Africa, from Dakar to French Equatorial Africa, and based on pidginized French;

6. the Kitchen-Kaffir which is a blend of Bantu, English, and Afrikaans, employed between native servants and their white masters in the South African Union;

7. the Oregon Trade language (also known as Chinook Jargon) which flourished on the American northwest coast as a means of communication between white traders and whalers and the Indians of several tribes (Nootka, Nisqually, Chihailish, Chinook, and others);

8. *Sabir*—a mixture of French, Spanish, Italian, Greek, and Arabic, used in some Mediterranean ports; and

9. the Spanish pidgin of the Philippines, still alive in a few areas.

The broad distribution and number of makeshift languages point to a universal need for intergroup communication. Again and again the pressure of this need breaks through language barriers and spontaneously creates linguistic structures which enable individuals and groups to bridge over to one another.

International Languages

There is nothing new or recent about the obstacles to intergroup communication created by the multiplicity of languages. The Tower of Babel myth is one of the oldest texts in the Old Testament. The natives of Australia have elaborate legends accounting for the creation of different languages by their totemic ancestors. Ancient Greeks nicknamed all foreign speakers stutterers or inarticulate, and most Slavic languages refer to the speakers of German as "mute." But to explain the origin of linguistic diversity or to express irritation with it is not enough. For often means have had to be devised for solving the problem of language differences.

The Indians of the American Plains hit upon a rather unusual solution when they evolved an intertribal sign language. The signs were made with the hands and fingers and referred only to ideas and never to the sounds of spoken words. The Crow, Kiowa, Arapaho, Cheyenne, and Blackfoot were considered among the most proficient in the use of this system of communication, which was also known to the Omaha, Osage, Kansas, and Ute.[6]

The Chinese system of writing shares with the Plains Indians' sign language the characteristic of disregarding the phonetic aspects of speech and that of using visual symbols which refer directly to ideas. Thus Mandarin-speaking Northerners and Cantonese-speaking Southerners in China who do not understand each others' speech can communicate in writing by means of their ideographic characters. In theory at least, the Chinese system of writing could be used for large-scale international communication, a possibility that was pointed out by Descartes in the seventeenth century.[7]

The most obvious way of meeting the problem of international communication is to adopt for this purpose any one of the existing languages of mankind. This method has been tried many times, often with quite effective results. Thus, Sumerian played this role in the ancient Near East as a link between the Babylonians, Assyrians, Hittites, and other nations. Greek functioned as an international language from the time of Alexander the Great, all through the Hellenistic period and the life span of the Byzantine Empire, until the fall of Constantinople in 1453. Subsequently, Latin served as the language of intergroup relations, not only under the Roman Empire, but more pointedly in the Middle Ages, when a semblance of European unity was maintained largely due to its existence. Also in medieval Europe, the Provençal of the Troubadours of the twelfth and thirteenth centuries was known over a vast area, was used by men like St. Francis of Assisi and at the court of England, and made for a community of moods and sentiments. Other European examples of international languages include the Italian of the Renaissance, the French of the *Grand Siècle* (seventeenth century) and the German of philosophy and science in the nineteenth century. Finally there is English as the rising international language of modern times. All of these have been instances of voluntarily adopted languages used widely in intercultural relations within the confines of Western civilization, and occasionally beyond. However, by the end of the last century, it became apparent that with the great increase in travel, trade, scientific exchange, and intercultural interdependence, a more drastic and uniform solution was needed. International rivalries militated against the adoption of any one of the major languages for official intergroup uses. Moreover it was felt that living languages were too rich in historical irregularities, local variants, and untranslatable idioms to serve as an international idiom. Why not then *construct* a simple, clear, and rational language? The idea was not altogether novel: Leibnitz more than two centuries earlier had spoken in favor of a new artificial language[8] and numerous similar projects had been advanced since that time.

The first of these projects to attract a large following was that of the Rev. F. Schleyer of Vienna, who named his language *Volapük*. The latter's adherents held three conventions and by 1889 claimed one million followers.

Much more successful was the international language of *Esperanto*, created by Dr. L. L. Zamenhof of Poland. Esperanto's grammar can be mastered in a few hours of study, its spelling follows the "one sound—one symbol" principle, and its vocabulary is based on the most widely shared roots of the major European languages. For some time, Esperanto received a good deal of official attention, being recognized, for example, by the International Telegraphic Union, the London and Paris Chambers of Commerce, and the League of Nations. It was taught in at least eighteen different countries. In 1907 an improved version of Esperanto was produced under the name of *Ido*. A few years earlier, Professor G. Peano of Italy had proposed a universal language which would be derived entirely from Latin freed of all its structural difficulties. He gave it the name of *Latino Sine Flexione* or *Interlingua*, and his address in this new language before a convention of classical scholars was received enthusiastically. Four further projects in international languages should be mentioned. In 1922 Edgar Wahl proposed a language based on the most widely shared European elements, which he called *Occidental*. In 1928 the famous Danish linguist Otto Jespersen came out with a proposal of his own under the name of *Novial*.

In 1929 the Swiss scholar René de Sausurre launched a new improved version of Esperanto which he termed *Nov-Esperanto*. Finally, at about the same time, two English scholars I. A. Richards and C. K. Ogden confronted the world with the possibility of using an English vocabulary reduced to 850 basic words. This simplified type of English would be known as *Basic English* and, according to its advocates, it could easily meet the problem of international communication.

The most recent developments in this domain have been connected with the activities of the International Auxiliary Language Association, known by the abbreviated name of IALA. IALA began a few years ago as a research project in international communication, but before long produced a new international language of its own for which Peano's name *Interlingua* was borrowed.

The theory underlying *Interlingua* claims that there is no need for constructing artificial languages for international use, since such a language already exists in the form of terms and idioms common to all the languages spoken by the carriers of our type of civilization. Interlingua then is not a new linguistic invention but rather is *abstracted* from the existing languages of Europe. This language is essentially a correlate of our western scientific culture. Its claim to universality is related to the fact that the universalist outlook itself is an inalienable part of the scientific tradition of the Occident. The conception of Interlingua also has close affinity with B. L. Whorf's theory of the Standard Average European (SAE), which he claims underlies our seeming linguistic diversity. The uniqueness and originality of Interlingua are revealed in the open admission of its strictly European or Occidental character. Interlingua is not an international language in the literal sense of the word, but a medium for the expression of the universalist message of the European intellectual tradition.

At this juncture in history, one hesitates to make any predictions regarding the future of universal languages. From past experience we note that they have met with far greater success in small and linguistically isolated nations such as Finland, Holland, Bulgaria, and Korea, than among the carriers of languages which already enjoy a worldwide distribution.

Footnotes to Chapter Six

1. Krieger, Herbert W.: *Peoples of the Philippines*, Washington, D.C., Smithsonian Institution, 1942, p. 61.

2. Webster, Noah: *Dissertations on the English Language*, Boston, 1789, p. 20.

3. The most up-to-date study of Haitian Creole is Hall, Robert J., Jr.: *Haitian Creole, Grammar, Texts, Vocabulary*, Menasha, Wisconsin, The American Anthropological Association, 1953, Vol. 55, No. 2, Part 2, Memoir No. 74.

4. For a brief profile of Mauritius Creole see Jespersen, Otto: *Language, Its Nature, Development and Origin*, New York, Henry Holt & Co., Inc., 1922, pp. 226–228.

5. The most recent scholarly study of Melanesian pidgin English is Hall, Robert Jr.: *Melanesian Pidgin English, Grammar, Texts, Vocabulary*, Baltimore, Md., Linguistic Society of America, 1943.

6. Clark, W. P.: *The Indian Sign Language*, Philadelphia, 1885.

7. Gode, Alexander: "The Case for Interlingua," *The Scientific Monthly*, 77:85 (August 1953).

8. *Ibid.*, p. 85.

chapter seven

Language and the Democratic Society

The earliest democracies of mankind, Athens, Iceland, and Switzerland, were all numerically small societies. Their size permitted their political deliberations to be open to all adult citizens. Furthermore, the issues with which they were concerned were usually within the narrow confines of their geographical existence. Thus political life was characterized by directness of participation and firsthand acquaintance with relevant information.

By contrast, the citizen of modern democracies feels remote from the seat of political power, dependent for knowledge on third parties, and often helpless in his ambition to contribute to the workings of his society. This situation creates a host of problems which must be met imaginatively if democracy is to preserve its vital characteristics.

One of these problems concerns the dissemination of information. It is obvious that any monopoly of communication is a threat to the democratic process.

Another problem has to do with the citizen's ability to interpret the information which is made available to him; he must evaluate its authenticity, relevance, and significance. There are dozens of good books dealing with verbal traps, logical fallacies, and the misuse of statistical information in public life. They have not thus far met with wide popular interest, in part at least a consequence of apathy which seems to be related to "bigness" in social and political life.

Democracy is also intimately wedded to the cultivation of individual preferences and choices in all walks of life. Mass production, mass consumption, mass education, and mass recreation are not always conducive to the growth of personalism.

There are numerous linguistic indices of this state of affairs. For example, the word *adjustment* has acquired an unquestioned positive conotation among many psychiatrists, social workers, and middle-class parents. The term *personality*, which in the past usually referred to individual idiosyncrasies and angularities, has come to mean the opposite of these traits. *Success* stresses the end product of individual activities and ignores their value or the means employed, just as we speak of best-sellers instead of good books. Even the term *sincere* recently has been given a new meaning far removed from its original use.

The scholar, the writer, and the artist must choose between remunerative catering to collective taste or the lonely pursuit of personal values. The unique and the experimental in arts and letters have become relegated to the anemic magazines of the avant-garde and emotional and verbal clichés have become objects of mass production.

A long-range plan of education aimed at strengthening the democratic way of life should, we believe, include the following objectives in the area of linguistic phenomena: the cultivation of immunity to emotion-laden but irrational appeals; training in semantic and logical analysis on a popular level; the encouragement of literary pioneering; a generous attitude toward regional speech differences; and a more encouraging attitude toward the languages of minority groups as vehicles for cultural variants. We hope that this short study contributes in some degree to these ends. But they must be undergirded by the emphatic restatement of the over-all importance of cultural pluralism and individual diversity as a foundation for the democratic philosophy of life.

Selected Readings

General Works on Language and Linguistics

Bloomfield, Leonard: *Language*, New York, Henry Holt, 1933.
The most scholarly and comprehensive treatment of the subject by one of the foremost American linguists.

Jespersen, Otto: *Language, Its Nature, Development and Origin*, London, Allen and Unwin, 1922.
A classic in the field of linguistics, particularly rich in suggestive historical illustrations of linguistic phenomena; obsolete in parts.

Sapir, Edward: *Language*, New York, Harcourt, Brace and Co., 1921.
A truly great book, less comprehensive than Bloomfield's but probably one of the most stimulating works on language ever written.

Sturtevant, Edgar H.: *An Introduction to Linguistic Science*, New Haven, Yale University Press, 1947.
A first-rate college text—clear, concise, and up-to-date.

On Alphabetic and Other Systems of Writing

Diringer, David: *The Alphabet, A Key to the History of Mankind*, 2nd ed., New York, Philosophical Library, 1953.
The best work on the subject.

Karlgren, Bernhard: *Sound and Symbol in Chinese*, London, Oxford University Press, 1923.
The best introduction to the nature of Chinese graphic symbolism; rich in theoretical implications.

Language and Philosophy

Ayer, Alfred Jules: *Language, Truth and Logic*, London, Victor Gollancz, 1947.
An excellent expression of the point of view of logical positivism.

Black, Max: *Language and Philosophy, Studies in Method*, Ithaca, N.Y., Cornell University Press, 1949.
A critical evaluation of the various philosophies of language.

Langer, Susanne K.: *Philosophy in a New Key*, New York, Penguin Books, 1948.

An original discussion of the nature of symbolic process; eminently readable.

Russell, Bertrand: *Human Knowledge, Its Scope and Limits*, New York, Simon and Schuster, 1948.
About one-fourth of this famous work deals with language.

Language and Literature

Duncan, Hugh Dalziel: *Language and Literature in Society*, Chicago, The University of Chicago Press, 1953.
An ambitious essay on the function of symbolism. Includes a bibliographical guide to the sociology of literature.

Pollock, Thomas Clark: *The Nature of Literature*, Princeton, N.J., Princeton University Press, 1942.
An excellent discussion of the relationship between literature and linguistics, and literature and semantics.

The Theory of Communication

Miller, George A.: *Language and Communication*, New York, McGraw-Hill Book Co., Inc., 1951.
The best statement of the behavioristic viewpoint; rich in empirical data.

Wiener, Norbert: *The Human Use of Human Beings*, A Doubleday Anchor Book, New York, Doubleday & Co., Inc., 1954.
A discussion of the field of cybernetics by its originator.

The School of General Semantics

Chase, Stuart: *Power of Words*, New York, Harcourt, Brace and Co., 1953.
A well-written popularization of the ideas of the school, as well as of other recent developments in this general area.

Hayakawa, S. I.: *Language in Thought and Action*, New York, Harcourt, Brace and Co., 1940.

Korzybski, Alfred: *Science and Sanity*, Lancaster, Pa., Science Press, 1933.
By the founder of the movement of general semantics.

The History of the English Language

Jespersen: *Growth and Structure of the English Language*, Oxford, England, Basil Blackwell, 1946.
A well-known classic.

Potter, Simeon: *Our Language*, Harmondsworth, Middlesex, England, Penguin Books, 1950.
A scholarly and lively portrayal of the English language with interesting data on modern trends.

Psychology of Language

Goldstein, Kurt: *Language and Language Disturbances*, New York, Grune and Stratton, Inc., 1948.

Bridges over from medical research to the theory of language.

Kasanin, J. S., ed.: *Language and Thought in Schizophrenia*, Berkeley, Cal., University of California Press, 1951.

Ten stimulating papers including those by H. S. Sullivan and N. Cameron.